Successful Spread Betting

Geoff Harvey

GLOBAL
professional
publishing

Global Professional Publishing
Random Acres
Slip Mill Lane
Hawkhurst
Cranbrook
Kent TN18 5AD

Email: publishing@gppbooks.com

Global Professional Publishing believes that the sources of information upon which the book is based are reliable, and has made every effort to ensure the complete accuracy of the text. However, neither Global Professional Publishing, the authors nor any contributors can accept any legal responsibility whatsoever for consequences that may arise from errors or omissions or any opinion or advice given.

ISBN 978-1-873668-58-0

Printed in the United Kingdom by Good News Press

Acknowledgements: Thank you to Emily Bulman and Vanessa Strowger for help and advice in preparation of the text.

You should seek professional advice before making any investments.

For full details of Global Professional Publishing titles in Finance, Banking see our website at:

www.gppbooks.com

Table of Contents

Foreword

The UK is home to the most highly developed sports gambling industry in the world. With a representative of the major bookmaking companies on virtually every high street and the option of placing bets by phone, it is easy to have access to an enormous choice of events to wager on at competitive prices.

The introduction of Spread Betting, itself a British innovation, presents the ultimate challenge to those interested in wagering on sports or the financial markets; a challenge that can promise winnings on a single trade of life changing proportions, though, if things go wrong, losses that are potentially life destroying.

The very mention of ëderivativesí, (the financial instruments that form the basis of Spread Betting), is liable to conjure up images of swaggering city traders capable of contributing vast sums to their companiesí coffers at the touch of a screen on a trading console. On the other hand it may bring to mind the extraordinary derivatives inspired collapse of the 800 year old merchant bank, Barings. For those not willing to take large financial risks, wins and losses can be broadly kept within preconceived limits, though, even if trading at the absolute minimum stakes allowed by Spread Betting firms, an average weekly wage can be won or lost on a couple of trades that are strikingly right or wrong.

My aim is to equip readers with the necessary insight into markets that will at least allow them to judge the potential of trades accurately. Betting in the UK has a high proportion of occasional gamblers who might risk a £3 each way bet on the Grand National, made on the basis of some spurious association with the names of their children; Spicing up a sporting event with a small wager is fine, but in general the levels of analysis required to be successful at Spread Betting are well in advance of those demonstrated most afternoons in betting shops up and down the country. It is not without reason that the spread companies are required by law to give a ëhealth warningí on their promotional material which alerts account holders of the high level of risk.

Warnings aside, Spread Betting offers potential rewards to those who know their sports that cannot be matched by traditional betting. If, through traditional betting, you were in the position of making a small profit over time, you might have to stake £1000 for every £100 you make as clear profit. Translate this sort of success rate to Spread Betting and your profits are likely to go through the roof very quickly. As an added incentive spread companies tend to tolerate winning clients more than the bookmakers, so there is less chance of having your bets lowered in stake, or refused.

This book should be of interest to those who already have spread accounts as well as those considering trying their hand at this exiting new form of gambling. It is useful for the reader to have a prior general knowledge of the principles of sports betting and to have a rough understanding of how the established fractional odds system works.

The concept of Spread Betting is comparatively simple. Two figures are quoted - you have a choice to bet higher than the high figure or lower than the low figure. Spread Betting is as simple or complex as you want it to be. If you wish to go into markets in detail you may find yourself spiralling into ever more complex mathematical considerations. For some this may be an enticing challenge, for others a tedious diversion. Some of the ideas I present here may look on the ëheavyí side but **no specialist mathematical knowledge is required** to understand them. An ability to work out the arithmetic mean of a set of numbers and a few percentages is really about as complicated as it gets.

Being capable of seeing a problem in a form that can be analysed using previous results and data is an advantage. If you are trying to work out how many goals might be scored in a live match between Liverpool and Newcastle, the task really comes down to assessing the relative importance of various pieces of information. Which is more significant, the fact that the two teams have produced a lot of goals in recent meetings or the fact that both sides have leading strikers out with injuries? An instinctive hunch about the situation may well pay off but taking the wrong decision on a spread bet is liable to cost a fair amount of money.

If you were considering buying some hi-fi equipment worth £300 you might want to take advice, ask questions and read a few consumer reports. If your football spread is potentially going to win/lose you that sort of sum of cash it is likewise advisable that you spend some time to undertake some form of meaningful research into the outcome before getting on the phone.

Although I have dedicated chapters to particular sports the ideas presented in each rarely apply only to the sport in question. Even if you personally concentrate on football you may well find ideas of interest in the chapter on racing that translate across. There are plenty of markets that are, in principle, related to one another, though they are on different sports. The *Time of First Goal* football market is the cousin of *Batsmen's Total Runs* in cricket, though on the face of it they appear to have little in common.

I have not attempted to give an exhaustive account of the rules that apply to Spread Betting. The rules governing markets vary between companies and these are covered in depth in their promotional literature. I have, however, tried to touch on some rules that lead to frequent misunderstandings. I have concentrated primarily on football and racing as these account for around 70% of spread bets. Rather than give cursory coverage to sports/markets I have absolutely no knowledge of I have taken the step of excluding them. My knowledge of, and interest in, American football (heavily touted by the spread firms) is just about nil and therefore I see no reason in pretending to be an expert.

My view on Spread Betting is necessarily a personal one; I am sure that many readers will disagree with my interpretation of markets. If I can fire up a few debates on the subject I would be very happy as, at present, there is only a limited ëSpread Betting cultureí in the UK. As the growth of Spread Betting is set to continue it is likely that information relating to, and discussion of, spread markets will increase. I hope that I have contributed to this process.

1 Origins and Principles

The ability to to trade 'in running' and to take an overall negative view on the participants are features of Spread Betting that makes it uniquely attractive.

The invention of sports Spread Betting in the UK is generally credited to the founder of the first Spread Betting company to open its doors, City Index. Jonathan Sparke and a companion, while in Paris for the 1981 Arc de Triomphe, dreamed up the concept of Spread Betting while wagering with each other on the aggregate card numbers of the horses finishing first and second. Sparke worked on refining this principle across a range of sports and two years later City Index took its first sports spread bet.

The principles of Spread Betting are closely associated with those of speculating on the financial markets, and indeed it wasnít until the entry of Sporting Index in 1987 that a company from outside the mainstream financial trading industry entered the sports betting market.

Spread Betting is based on the concept of financial derivatives. These have a legitimate and vital role in finance, though the public may associate them solely with high risk speculation for the sake of it. Imagine you are a small business buying goods from Austria and selling them in the UK. You pay for the goods in Austrian Schillings of which there are say 20 to the pound. Your profit margin is 20%. So long as the exchange rate remains the same, your profit should remain stable at around 20%. You are, however, vulnerable to fluctuations between the value of the two currencies. If the pound were to strengthen, leaving the exchange rate just 18 Sch. to the pound your profit margin would be slashed by around 50%. Unless you actually buy vast amounts of Austrian currency at present to finance future purchases you are at the mercy of potentially catastrophic currency fluctuations.

The only way of insuring against such an eventuality is to strike a deal with a trader which is ëderivedí from the underlying currency. Such a trade might involve being paid a sum by the trader for every Schilling that the rate drops below a predetermined threshold, and conversely, paying the trader when rates rise. In effect this means that in the unfortunate event of your business being hit by a drop in value of the Schilling then you have a compensatory payment as a result of the trade. If the rate rises you are liable to pay the trader, however your profits will have correspondingly increased so this shouldnít place a heavy financial burden. Hence a ëderivativeí trade has solved a genuine market problem.

In reality financial derivatives take on complex forms with bizarre naming systems. You are welcome to take a dive into the world of ëEgyptian Ratchetsí and ëTarantulasí if you so wish; though some derivatives strategies can be modified for Spread Betting purposes the conceptual gap between the financial and sporting markets is large.

Newcomers to Spread Betting may be forgiven for assuming that the basics are difficult to pick up, though it could be argued that traditional odds are far more bewildering for the beginner. The fractional odds that dominates betting in this country is almost designed to put people off. A system in which odds of 5/2 are followed in turn by 11/4 and 3/1 is not exactly accessible. It must be the hope of the Spread Betting companies that they will directly attract those new to any form of gambling rather than simply converting those used to the traditional form of odds.

Total Numbers

Spread Betting relies on the fact that sporting events are generally determined by a variable such as goals in football, and runs in cricket. In its most basic form, Spread Betting allows wagers on the these events occurring. The spread itself is essentially the firms prediction of the likely outcome. At the beginning of a test innings by the West Indies the spread may be quoted as:

West Indies, first innings runs   300 - 320

Here the firm is inviting two types of bets; from those who think the total will be higher than 320 and those who feel it will end up lower than 300. If you are inclined to think that the spread looks too high and decide to bet, you would choose your unit stake (say £1), pick up the phone and ëstrikeí a trade. For every run that the West Indies finish below 300 you are paid £1 by the firm. For every run they achieve over 300 you lose £1. So if their final score is 238 you win £62 (300-238 = 62). Should they manage a total of 321 then you lose £21.

- **Going lower than the quote is always termed 'selling'** (in this case, under 300),

- **Going higher than the quote is always termed 'buying'** (in this case, 320).

Your trade, in the above example, would therefore be, ìSell West Indies first innings runs at 300 for £1 per runî.

The first quote may be available at 10.50am, ten minutes before the opening over is bowled. If there are a lot of other account holders striking buy trades, (for instance if the pitch report states that it is drier and flatter than expected), then the spread (displayed on Teletext) might move up to 310-330. And this is without the players even coming onto the field. When the game commences the batsmen put on nine, then a wicket falls.

The original estimate of 310-330 now looks too high. The quote lowers immediately to 270-290. You are in a position to close the trade at a profit. As you sold at 300 you could now buy at 290 for £1. This closes the original trade and leaves you with a profit of £10. The final score of the innings is now immaterial - if the innings was to close at 200 you would technically have won £100 on your sell trade and lost £90 on your buy trade. The same profit of £10 is gained whether the final score is 57 or 600.

Closing a trade is an option at any time during play in this particular cricket market. So if the openers cracked 50 without loss in a handful of overs and the spread had jumped to 340-360, you could give the bet up as a bad job, buy at 360, taking a £60 loss before things got even worse.

The final ëresultí of the market is termed the ë**make-up**í. So in this example if the innings closes at 293 all out, the make-up is deemed to be 293. The ëmake-upí of a market should be distinguished from the actual ëresultí of the sporting contest. If you bet on the number of corners in a football match between Chelsea and Arsenal the ëmake-upí is the final tally of corners, say 12, whereas the ëresultí is perhaps a 1-1 draw.

The importation of the phrases ëbuyí and ësellí from financial trading is, in some ways, unfortunate. The concept that you can ësellí something that you didnít ëbuyí in the first place is usually the first sticking point for those considering Spread Betting. The expressions ëgo lowí and ëgo highí are perhaps easier to understand for the beginner.

Supremacy

The degree to which one competitor will beat another is the basis for a second category of spread bets. An example of this type of ërelative performanceí market would be on a tennis match between Sampras and Pioline. Here you might see a quote expressed simply as:

```
                      Sampras/Pioline 3 - 4
```

The quote is measured in games. In a football match a similar ërelative performanceí quote would refer to goals; in snooker, frames. If you think Sampras will win by more than four games you would buy at four. If the match goes 6-4, 6-4, 6-3 Sampras has achieved a supremacy of seven games (he has won seven games more than Pioline). You would therefore win the difference between seven and four, multiplied by your stake. It may be the case that Sampras loses by three games. In this case his supremacy ëmakes-upí at minus three. As a buyer you would lose the difference between four and minus three (7) multiplied by your stake. This type of bet may be applied to a number of sports, hence a golf quote of Woosnam/Janzen 1.5 - 2.0 applies to the number of shots that Woosnam is expected to beat Janzen by.

In these supremacy bets one may come across a quote of -0.5yc. The ë**yc**í stands for ë**your choice**í and offers you the chance to buy either of the named competitors at - 0.5. This occurs when both competitors are rated as having an equal chance. You cannot sell either competitor; buying their opponent is effectively the same.

Performance Index

The third *distinct* form of spread bets are the artificial ëindicesí. Here the make-ups are determined not by actual sporting events but by allocating points depending on performance. An index on the FA Cup may award points on the following basis:

>   Win = 100 points
>   Runner Up = 70 points
>   Semi-finalist = 50 point
>   Quarter finalists = 33 points
>   Last sixteen = 10 points
>   Others = 0

```
Liverpool  35-38
```

If you were to buy at £2 and Liverpool won the Cup they are assigned 100 points. You would, therefore, win the difference between 100 and 38 (62 points) multiplied by your stake of £2 = £124. If they only reached the last sixteen you would lose the difference between 38 and 10 (28 points multiplied by your stake of £2 = £56).

Gearing

The concept of ëgearingí is central to Spread Betting. On a bicycle the gear selected determines the relationship between the number of revolutions of the pedal and the number of revolutions of the wheel. In a high gear a small movement of the pedals produces a disproportionately large movement in the wheel.

In betting terms, if a small variation in the score or result of a game cause a huge fluctuation in the amount you can win or lose then this would be an example of a highly geared bet. Traditional fractional bets generally display low gearing, a low ratio between the stake and the possible win or loss. A bet on Aston Villa to win their home game at odds of 4/5 means that you can either win 180% of your initial stake of lose 100% of the stake. Spread Betting, (where many times your initial stake are risked on events that may be comparatively insignificant to the overall result of the sporting contest), display varying degrees of gearing.

The number of goals in a football match rarely exceeds six so on a *Total Goals* market the range of possible outcomes is reasonably low. The most heavily geared market generally available is probably *Test Match Innings Runs* in cricket which realistically can be anywhere between 70 and 800. Hence even at a very modest sounding £2 per run you could potentially be looking at a profit or loss of more than £1,000. For those looking for a real rollercoaster ride the most heavily geared market, and therefore the one with most risk attached is on *Total Test Match Series Runs*, where one can expect a quote somewhere in the 6,000ís.

Occasionally spread companies deliberately increase the gearing by multiplying two variables together. Hills offer a football quote on *Multi Corners* based on the number of corners scored in the first half multiplied by those in the second half. Normally the corners market is fairly sedate with a low volatility - conceivably the make-up for a game would be between 3 and 22. So, whether as a buyer or a seller, the vast majority of matches would see a potential profit/loss of +/- 10 points. The effect of multiplying the first half tally by the second increases the gearing enormously. Now the potential make-ups fall within a range of 0 - 121.

Features

The ability to take an overall **negative view** on the participants is the feature of Spread Betting that makes it uniquely attractive. Before the advent of Spread Betting it was virtually impossible to have a wager that supports a view that a certain participant would do badly. For instance, you might feel that Tiger Woods was being hyped by the media too much and the prospects of him winning a particular tournament were being overestimated. In this case you would be set with the near impossible task of backing potential winners other than Woods himself (which in a field of more than 100 competitors at many golf tournaments is a fairly thankless task). Today with a simple spread bet you could strike a trade on his finishing position and sit back in the knowledge that you have the rest of the field playing for you.

The ability to trade ëin runningí (as the event is in progress) is the second major feature of Spread Betting. Previously, the moment your betting slip was rung through the till of a bookmaker it was set in stone. There could be no other decision to make - just let the event run its course.

Betting in running effectively lets you delay a wager until play has started, change your mind half way through or, for that matter, make a reasoned judgement based on the state of play that it is wiser not to bet at all. Inevitably the spread companies are heavily dependent on live TV action and it is on these events where trading is at its most brisk. The fact that quotes are available on both Teletext and Skytext and can be displayed ëin visioní (a section of a companyís Teletext page constantly updating in the top corner of the TV screen) still further enhances the attraction of betting in running.

It should be noted that the price you see on the screen is not necessarily the price you get. The slightest change in events on the field of play can influence the overall result, and therefore the quote. Try buying a football teamís supremacy when they are about to take a penalty and you are likely to be disappointed at the quote you receive.

Spread Betting enjoys an **enviable tax position**. At present all off-course ëtraditionalí bets are subject to a levy of 9% which is made up of gaming tax and a contribution to the Horse Racing Levy Board. This 9% (though a reduction from the previous 10%) is the stumbling point of most serious gamblers. On any one bet the punter has to overcome a margin that the bookmaker has built into the odds of at least 10%. This is just about attainable over the long term for a small percentage of gamblers. But, life is made doubly difficult by the imposition of the 9% tax and this added hurdle contributes to the fact that the numbers of high staking ëprofessionalí gamblers in this country probably numbers less than 100. Spread Betting tax is 5% and only paid on the unit stake, a sum so small on the vast majority of trades that the spread companies absorb the cost themselves. This gives the serious spread bettor a massive advantage over his traditional wagering counterpart.

Spread Betting, where oneís losses are not finite, is subject to a new type of regulatory framework. Traditional bookmaking debts on either side are not enforceable by law. It may come as a surprise to some that if Ladbrokes decided not to pay you out on a legitimate bet you cannot go to court to claim your winnings. Spread Betting debts are, however, enforceable. You can sue and be sued. If you have a particularly bad nightmare on the 3.20 at Newmarket then your house may be sold to pay off the debt - a sobering thought. Spread Betting is regulated in the UK by the Securities and Futures Authority (SFA) who act as a financial ëwatchdogí.

The Players

S pread Betting ëcame of ageí in early 1997 with the entry of *Ladbrokes* into the market who set up a division separate from their traditional bookmaking activities. This ëblessingí by the biggest name in British gambling bought the total of companies to five alongside the originators *City Index, IG Index, Sporting Index* and *Hills Index*. Like most affluent ëcreatures of the eightiesí the spread companies were hard hit by the early 1990ís recession but today Spread Betting is estimated to enjoy 15% of total betting turnover. It has to be said that it certainly doesnít account for 15% of bets placed; spread bettors are comparatively few (approximately 20,000 accounts) but they have a good deal of money to throw around.

In July 1998 *Ladbrokes* bowed out of the Spread Betting market, selling their client list to *IG Index*. For account holders this is both good and bad news. The fact that Ladbrokes found it tough to maintain a profit suggests that spread companies are not fallible and that account holders have every chance to make money from them. On the other hand the demise of their Spread Betting operation means less competition in the market which can only be against the interests of all account holders.

Football heads the list of the most popular sports to bet on with over 40% of turnover. Racing follows with another 25-30% though its share is declining. This is perhaps not surprising seeing the huge increase in the amount of televised live football recently coupled with the fact that racing is finding it difficult to attract enthusiasts from younger generations. At present Spread Betting is inevitably popular amongst those who trade for a living anyway and remains fairly London dominated in terms of account holders. For some reason, journalists are disproportionately represented among account holders which must occasionally cause alarm bells as one would imagine that sports journalists in particular would be frequently privy to information not available to the spread companies.

Spread Betting has so far avoided any major match fixing or corruption scandal, though it has to be said that where there is money to be made on such a scale it is likely that a few individuals closely connected with sport must be tempted to manipulate results unfairly. Perhaps the publicity that results from any future ëcoupsí will be worth more to the spread companies than the losses on the market itself. The only real evidence of fishy goings on concerned the *Time of the First Throw in* market on football. The companies themselves kicked this market into touch following a number of high profile incidents including, most notably, the highly suspicious actions of West Hamís Paul Kitson in booting the ball out of play straight from the kick off at the start of a match with Manchester United. Kitson probably did us all a favour by helping to rid us of the ëTime of the First Throw marketí, which was trivial in the extreme.

All the companies are attempting to broaden the appeal of Spread Betting and minimum stakes are falling constantly in a bid to attract a wide cross section of sports fans. *Sporting Index* operate a ëSelect ë account where losses on all trades are guaranteed not to exceed £50 when betting at the minimum stakes. New innovations are likely. City Index are teaming up with *Sporting Life/Press Association Group* to bring Spread Betting onto the Internet, and other companies could be persuaded to enter the fray. Spread Betting is expected to be launched in Australia, Singapore and Hong Kong shortly. More companies means more markets and better choice of prices for account holders. Sporting spreads are undoubtedly with us to stay.

2 Inspiration v Analysis

Spread Betting study time is often rewarded - account holders who are in profit have reached their position generally at the expense of those who have turned to spread betting as a fun diversion.

Inspiration

One particular summers night sticks in my memory. At 2am I had more or less given up on trying to get to sleep. Once before that summer I had a similarly uncomfortable night having opened a spread trade on innings runs where I had predicted the England innings to be higher than the quote. The rain poured down incessantly for over eight hours and it looked as though the England innings, along with a few hundred pounds of mine, would be washed away. This time however my insomnia was due to the terrific heat and humidity, more akin to the Borneo jungle than a summer night in West London. As I laboured down the stairs for a cocoa, or something stronger, I paused to open a window, only to find that the air that came wafting in was disconcertingly hotter than that in the house. For some reason, at this time in the morning I tend to find myself considering upcoming Spread Betting opportunities and on this occasion began thinking about the consequences of the weather on the Sixth Test match between England and Australia due to get under way at the Oval in the morning.

The relationship between the physics, the weather and the performance of batsmen in cricket is very much at the boundaries of known science. The BBCís ëTomorrowís Worldí comes back to the subject every five years or so. On the last occasion they declared that in the fractions of a second it takes for a cricket ball to hurtle 22 yards towards a batsmen human reaction time was not quick enough to even vaguely be able to make out where the ball was heading, let alone play a majestic drive to the third man boundary. Why a cricket ball swings around in mid air, causing the batsmen to miss it completely or edge it towards the slip fieldsmen is similarly open to question. Cricket commentators tend to point to cloud cover and humidity as the main contributory factors though steer away from any detailed discussion of the precise aerodynamic principles that are at work.

It was fairly obvious that the humidity was intense and that I was not the only person suffering. My interest in the potential of opening a bet that predicted that not many runs would be scored was sustained by the knowledge that the TV commentators and press had been consistently predicting that the Oval pitch would be flat and lifeless and hence perfect for scoring plenty of runs. The temperature was plainly going to be in the region of 90 degrees in the morning (always said to favour the batting side) and I was well aware that any hint of a good chance of runs galore would see plenty of individuals wagering on high batting scores. Therefore, if I was to go against the crowd and predict that the batsmen would face testing conditions with a ball swerving around in the air I was going to get a good price for my wager.

A total of 4943 runs had been scored in the previous five test matches, with Australia already having retained the Ashes. I considered selling the current quote of 6125. Effectively I was saying that the total runs scored in the final Test would be lower than 1182 (the difference between the 4943 that had already been scored and the spread firms ëpredictedí overall total of 6125). With 1182 runs to play with this meant that there had to be an average of 295 runs per innings; this I considered was on the generous side and decided to go along with my humidity theory and make a trade. In the event I didnít have to wait long before knowing that my hunch that runs would be at a premium was correct.

England batted first and slumped to 180 all out. Australia managed 220 in reply and England then followed with a second innings of only 163. Australia could only muster 104 in their final innings (for which they spectacularly lost the match) the total runs for the test was just 667, leaving me with 515 points in profit.

I really donít know whether it was the humidity that contributed to the low scores. Iíve since learned that an eminent professor dismisses the ëhumidity = swingí theory entirely. Shane Warne inflicted appalling damage on the England card with his vicious spin bowling which has more do with his ability to get the ball to turn off the ground, though it was acknowledged that the ball did more in the air than was expected. In any case, I was certainly glad to have gone against the opinions of others who were backing a high scoring match.

The central point behind this tale is that some successful spread trades are made on the basis of a very simple premise that doesnít require any particular expertise, long computer analysis or a higher degree in probability theory. However there are times when it pays to sit down and work through a betting opportunity from scratch.

Analysis

At the other end of the analytical spectrum from the Test match example was a headache inducing problem that I encountered with a spread on the team that scores the most goals in a selection of Premiership matches:

Arsenal	16 - 19
Liverpool	14 - 17
Manchester Utd.	13 - 16
Blackburn	11 - 14
Newcastle	9 - 12
West Ham	7 - 9
Coventry	5 - 7

First   = *50 points*
Second = *25 points*
Third   = *10 points*

In this Index the seven teams are playing on the same afternoon against various opponents (these are not listed). Your challenge is to predict which team will score the most goals in their game. The team who scores the most is assigned 50 points, so if you buy Blackburn at 14 and they end up putting six goals past Derby, (collecting the 50 points), you are paid the difference between 50 and 14 (36) multiplied by your stake.

I was particularly interested in this Index because I tend to think that people generally overestimate the superiority of so called ëgoodí teams.

I really wanted to find out whether the difference in prices between the top team on the spread (on my example Arsenal) and the bottom team (Coventry) were really justified. Did the ëgoodí teams really score more goals than the unfancied teams to the extent suggested by the spreads?

In the example letís say Arsenal are at home to Southampton whilst Coventry are away at Wimbledon. Even the most partisan Southampton follower would have to concede that Arsenal have a better chance of scoring more goals against Southampton than Coventry do away at Wimbledon. Buying Arsenal at 19 looks to be an excellent bet. They have the ëeasiestí looking match of all the seven teams and the possible gain is 36 points as compared to a potential loss of only 19. On the other hand I was suspicious of the difference between the quotes on the teams and began wondering whether a consistent policy of selling the team with the highest quote might reap long term rewards. But how can all this be quantified ?

The only way of really assessing this Index would be to keep a log of the indices each week with the results and see what the consequences of selling or buying all the teams quoted with the highest prices. As the index is only offered at weekends it would take around three years to accumulate enough evidence to decide one way or the other. This was clearly impractical so I decided to ëmodelí results on previous fixtures. This technique is fairly simple in principle, though in this case became quite involved. Firstly, I first had to find a way of quantifying how good the seven teams in the Index were in relation to each other.

To do this I had to look no further than the fixed odds prices of the teams involved. Arsenal were 4/7 favourites to beat Southampton. Liverpool were 4/5 to beat Tottenham etc. down to the other end of the favouritism scale, Coventry, who were 13/8 to win at Wimbledon.

If I had a large number of results of teams playing at these odds I could construct a number of ëfantasyí indices based on matches whose results I already knew. It didnít matter who the teams were, or who or when they played. I could pitch a team who were 4/7 against a team who was 4/5 and other teams at odds corresponding to those in the original index. It was then a short step to seeing how the 4/7 rated team performed if the same points assigning system were used (50 for the team who scored most, 25 for second and 10 for 3rd).

For exactly these sorts of purposes I keep results of matches on the bookmakers printed football betting slips going back over a period of about five years. On a particular day Liverpool might have been 4/7 to beat Bolton. They would head my ëfantasyí index with a spread of 16-19. On perhaps another day entirely Manchester United would be 4/5 to beat Sheffield Wednesday. They would be assigned a spread of 14 - 17. It is all too easy, when constructing these sort of models, toí twistí the gathering of data in a way which fits your theory. One has to have a rigorous set of rules regarding exactly which matches are to be included in the model. This exceedingly time consuming exercise, logging 546 results (seven for each index), yielded a total of 78 ëfantasyí indices one of which is reproduced here.

Fixed odds price	Implied spread	Number of goals scored	Implied result of Index
4/7	(16 - 19)	1	0 points
8/13	(14 - 17)	1	0 points
4/6	(13 - 16)	2	10 points
8/11	(11-14)	3	25 points
4/5	(9 - 12)	4	50 points
11/8	(7 - 9)	0	0 points
13/8	(5 - 7)	0	0 points

Remember this is not a real index, just one cobbled together from previous unrelated results. On this occasion the team rated at 4/5, when randomly put up against other teams at different prices, ëwoníand would have been assigned 50 points. On its own this index is fairly meaningless - it is a tiny snapshot of the larger picture.

However, if one has enough of such examples it becomes possible to make generalisations about the performances of the teams in relation to their prices. My sample of 78 ëfantasyí indices is *possibly* a little too low to be absolutely conclusive, but nevertheless gave some fairly clear results.
Buying the teams at the higher prices is utterly fruitless. But if you were to sell the highest rated team at 16 on every single occasion, you seemed to amass a profit of 236 points. This despite the occasions when the 16-19 rated team did, in fact, clearly score the most goals and get 50 points assigned. This profit divided by the 78 trials suggested that, on average, there was a three point profit to be had every time you sold the top rated team. Having completed the theoretical element I sat

back and watched the Index over the next few weeks and, indeed, the actual results appeared to mirror what I had predicted. Over 15 weeks there appeared to be an average of a three point gain every time you sold the top rated team.

Watching the prices move over the Saturday that the games were held, I realised that there was a tendency for the top rated teams to move up a couple of points, indicating that there were plenty of people who believed that buying the top team was good value.

I think I had collected enough evidence to suggest that, in fact, the exact opposite was true; the value was in selling these sides, particularly near to kick-off when their prices were at their highest. As long as this situation holds, Iím selling the top rated club on the Index as a matter of routine.

The Debate

There is a vast contrast between the many hours of work it took to look at the football example and the apparent flash of inspiration in the test match cricket. I donít include them to demonstrate that I have a constant record of winning trades (which I certainly donít); however it is worth bearing in mind whenever you make a trade the quality and depth of the information you are basing it on.

There are many issues left totally unresolved in betting. Many debate subjects endlessly, though few actually sit down and bother to work out the underlying truth. I always thought it was common knowledge that so many people bet on favourites ëthrough the cardí on the Tote Placepot that on the occasions the favourites were all placed the dividend was paltry and considerably lower than the SP equivalent. Recently, however, Nick Mordin in his excellent gambling book *Betting For a Living* repeats a theory that favourites are underrepresented in Placepot entries and that favourites through the card is an excellent value wager. Who should one believe? Apart from the need to have access to huge amounts of race results the analysis of this problem would be very involved and time consuming. I have no doubt that with Spread Betting study time is often rewarded - account holders who are in profit have reached their position generally at the expense of those who have turned to Spread Betting as a fun diversion.

3 Account Management

Though it goes without saying that you should thoroughly understand the rules governing any particular market before trading on it, there are a number of pitfalls that are not obvious at first sight.

Opening a Spread Betting account is relatively straightforward. Ring any of the Freephone numbers operated by spread companies and youíll be sent an information pack and application form. Fierce competition for new accounts recently has meant that companies are offering a number of incentives. This often takes the form of a free bet, for instance a £50 per *Goal Supremacy* bet on a major football game - you keep any winnings but are not liable for any losses. As there are, on the face of it, only minor differences in the competing firms the relative value of these promotions is well worth looking into for anyone considering opening an account.

Some basic financial details are required and you are likely to be asked to supply evidence of your financial standing in the form of bank/building society statements etc. But it would be wrong to assume that only the well off are given accounts. Self employment or tenant status are no bar to opening an account providing you can demonstrate sufficient funds and the process is remarkably quick. They want your business, so you can expect to receive your trading number (that which identifies you when making trades) within a few days of sending off the form.

The actual financial management of accounts varies between companies. The easiest is to have the account managed by debit card whereby winnings are credited (and losses debited) automatically at the end of each accounting period (from one week to one month). You should be set some form of limit on your trades though this tends to be flexible. If you have deposited, for example, £500, you are unlikely to be permitted to trade at levels where your potential liabilities exceed this figure. With a credit account there is no need to lodge a deposit and accounts are settled both ways by cheque shortly after the end of each accounting period, which is generally weekly or bi-weekly. The company sends a full statement detailing the weekís trades and your overall position; it is also possible to receive a separate confirmation note of each trade placed.

All conversations with traders are recorded should there be any future dispute. When making a trade you first quote your account number and then ask for the quote on the market you are interested in. If the quote is to your liking you simply state your trade i.e. ìSell Manchester United supremacy at 2.1 for £30î. The trader then repeats back what he understands to be your trade and you need to correct immediately if it is not what you intended.

It is worth knowing at exactly what point the trade is completed. This is generally when the trader confirms that the trade is logged. This varies slightly from company to company. It can be on the word ë**done**í when the trader says, ìthatís done for youî. This is vital if you are betting in running as an event can happen suddenly that can effect the quote dramatically. If, whilst you are in the process of making a trade on a football match a goal is scored, you want to be absolutely sure you donít get into a dispute over whether the trade was completed or not.

All trades you complete should be written down. I keep a simple log of each trade alongside the precise time (to the nearest minute) it was made. Should any dispute occur you are obliged to provide a fairly exact time of the trade.

Statements must be rigorously checked against your record of trades and their results. Mistakes do occur occasionally. I am very much in favour of pointing out any mistakes that are made in the account holders favour. The legendary gambler Alex Bird recounts that one of the only bookmakers who consistently accepted his bets was a firm to which he had pointed out an error in the their favour. If you own up to a mistake in a spread companiesí favour I assume any future mistakes that are against you will be handled in a favourable light. In addition you tend to be ërewardedí when owning up with a free bet or favourable price on your next trade.

Knowing Your Markets

Timing

Though it goes without saying that you should thoroughly understand the rules governing any particular market before trading on it, there are a number of pitfalls that are not obvious at first sight. Of primary importance is knowing at what times you can trade on a chosen market. Imagine you have had a bet on a golf tournament. You sit back and watch the highlights on TV at 9pm and to your joy discover that you are nearing a ìstop winî position. You decide to close out the bet. But when? The spread companies office is closed and doesnít reopen until 9.30am the next day. The golfers will be well into the next dayís round by then and the market is not updated in running, therefore you have to sit and sweat it out, losing your option to close the trade.

The actual opening hours of firms vary from day to day, often depending on whether there is live sport in the evening. Certain times are much busier than others, so if you want a detailed explanation of an obscure rule in the greyhound index its best not to phone during half time of the FA Cup Final.

Make-up

The rules which govern make-ups are not always transparently obvious. Take another golfing scenario in which there is an index on the leading golfers of a tournament. The index awards 50 points for the winner 25 for second and 10 for third. The final scores look like this:

Tiger Woods	268	
Davis Love III		269
Nick Faldo		269
Phil Mickelson		270
Constantino Rocca		270

There are a number of ways people tend to make errors in this situation. The most common misinterpretation would be to award Woods 50 for coming first, splitting the 25 available for second between Love and Faldo who are tied (awarding them 12.5 points each) and again splitting the third place between Mickelson and Rocca (awarding them five points each).The error here is to think in terms of Love and Faldo sharing second place. They are in fact sharing second and third places (worth a total of 35 points), therefore the correct make-up is:

Tiger Woods	50
Davis Love III	1 7
Nick Faldo	1 7
Others	0

Ticks & Points

A potentially very nasty misunderstanding can arise in the difference between ëticksí and ëpointsí. On any index involving goals, for example, the quote is expressed in tenths of a goal, hence a 2.4 - 2.7 *Total Goals* quote. A tick is the smallest unit the market is traded in - here tenths of a goal. An instruction to sell total goals at £50 a point can potentially be interpreted as £50 per goal or tenth of a goal. If you mean the trade to be in whole goals itís going to come as something of a shock to discover it has been booked as £50 per tick, in which case you are slumbering in you chair blissfully unaware that you have a cool £500 per goal wager in running.

As a general rule always describe trades in whatever unit you mean. If you want £50 per goal, actually say ëper goalí not simply ëper pointí or even just ësell for £50í. If you make enough trades during your gambling life and arenít absolutely clear what you mean on each and every occasion you could find a potentially catastrophic situation just round the corner.

Multiple Bets

The choice of markets on all sports is increasing at a furious pace. You will be aware that in betting shops you only see a handful of bets actively promoted. This are generally the multiple bets with alluring names like ëSuper Yankeeí or ëGoliathí. The reason the bookmakers promote these bets is that there is a higher profit margin to be had in them. The more multiple bets placed, in whatever exotic form, the more profit for the bookmaker. In Spread Betting the promotion of markets is slightly more subtle. There are no multiple bets as such but the ideal situation for the spread companies is that individuals bet with them on markets where the results are basically down to chance and little or no advantage can be gained by having any particular knowledge of what one is betting on.

Imagine a spread market on the great statisticiansí recourse of coin flipping - an entirely random event. The bookmaker is able to calculate the indisputably correct odds in an instant. Thousands of eager punters place their bets on the outcome. None of them can possibly have a long term advantage over another. They are all equal hostages to statistical fortune and, if there is the usual margin built into the odds, they should all lose equally in the long run.

A market on a proper sporting event where knowledge and skill can be put to good use is different. Some backers will have an advantage over others and may start wagering heavily. The initial odds offered can only be an estimate - they cannot be based on the ëtrueí chances of the individual competitors.

Essentially spread companies would love us to wager consistently on markets where pure chance is the overriding factor. Particularly heavily promoted are the weekend multi-indices. As well as being very prominent on the Teletext pages they are also analysed in the racing press. These generally have six or even more components covering a variety of sports. **To attempt to end up ahead in these markets is folly**. I confess that these indices always manage to catch the eye but the components are generally deliberately obscure. Mixing a live TV gameís Shirt Numbers with the performance of a driver in the Grand Prix, the number of rounds a fighter will last in a boxing match, and heaven knows what else, soon becomes the Spread Betting equivalent of flipping a coin.

The Winning Edge

Most gamblers are heartily sick of hearing the mantra ë*the book-maker always wins*í. This depressing phrase reflects the fact that, mathematically, bookmakers should beat their clients over time. A set of odds on an event will include a profit margin so that if the bookmakers are guaranteed to payout less money than they take on bets.

There is a lot of rather misleading ways of gauging how good or bad a gambler is. Frequently one hears of boasts of level stakes profits or high strike rates, particularly with tipping services and premium rate phone lines. All to often these are smokesreens for what is in fact a losing position. There is only one way of fairly reporting on a gamblerís performance. This is by taking total winnings as a percentage of total stakes. In traditional betting the formula looks like this:

$$\text{Total stake } = £ \ 986$$
$$\text{Total win } \ = £1028$$

$$\frac{1028}{986} \times 100 = 104.26\%$$

On these you win back just over 4% of what he staked.

With Spread Betting you would simply express performance as ëwins as a percentage of lossesí. A 100% performance would indicate that the account holder won exactly the same as he lost:

$$\text{Total lost } = £1576$$
$$\text{Total won } = £1348$$

$$\frac{1348}{1576} \times 100 = 85.53\%$$

Here you would incur an overall loss of just over 15%. This percentage should, if the bookmakers have it their way, broadly reflect the margin that they have built into their odds. In fractional betting the margin varies considerably depending on the event. In general the more possible outcomes the more margin there is in the bookmakers favour. So a tennis match between Stark and Henman can only result in two possible outcomes (a victory for either player).

If you were offered 5/6 on both players (each a 54.55% chance) the percentages add up to 109.1% (See appendix for an explanation of how fractional odds are converted to percentages). If you bet on such terms consistently and displayed no particular talent for picking tennis winners you can expect to lose around 10% of your total stakes (ignoring the tax element of the bet). In a 10 runner horse race the total percentages of the odds are likely to be something in the region of 125%, a 150 entry golf tournament at least 150%.

The ëaverageí gambler wins back around 75% of his stakes. This assumes he bets only on singles. He loses 15% because of the bookmakers margins and in addition pays off course tax (currently standing at 9%). Anyone venturing into the world of multiple bets (doubles and trebles) is at a disadvantage as the bookmakers margin built into the odds starts multiplying rapidly through the different stages of a multiple bet. Indiscriminately placing trebles on horse meetings or football coupons is liable to win back less than 40% of your stake over time.

The position with Spread Betting is considerably more favourable. Working out the margin to overcome can be a little tricky because it is not always clear what the range of possible outcomes are. In our fractional odds tennis example there are clearly only two outcomes but in many spread markets, (such as *Total Cricket Innings Runs*), any estimate of the range of make-ups is open to debate. Perhaps the easiest way to get an idea of margins is to examine a simple performance index where there is a definite cap on what can be won or lost.

Woods	18 - 21
Els	14 - 17
Westwood	11 - 14
Olazabal	10 - 13
Faldo	8 - 11
Woosnam	8 - 11
Goosen	6 - 8

Win = 50
Second = 25
Third = 10
Only these seven count

On this index the range of results is known. Only the seven named players can be awarded points and we can easily tell how many points are being contested. Adding all the available points up (50 + 25 + 10) we arrive at a total points award of 85. A simple test to tell what the margin in favour of the spread firm stands at for this index is to look at the consequence of backing all the possible outcomes. Imagine we were to buy all the players for £1. The total of all seven buy prices is 95 therefore to break even we would have to win 95 points from somewhere. Clearly this is impossible as there are only 85 on offer. So for our stake of £95 we must lose £10. This deficit represents a theoretical margin in favour of the spread firm of more than 10%.

This figure of just over 10% is fairly standard across all Spread Betting markets and is considerably lower than that which has to be overcome by a fractional odds gambler on most bets. Spread companies can afford to be slightly more generous with their margins as bets are all placed by telephone, overcoming the need to rent and staff premises.

In addition the average spread account holder risks considerably greater sums, whereas shop staff frequently have to toil away at settling 5p each-way Yankees. However the gearing on Spread Betting means that a ë10% lossí takes on frightening proportions when it comes to adding up the actual pennies.

Whenever you place a bet you are effectively being ërobbedí of the difference between the midpoint of the quote and the figure you traded at. If you sell the quote of *Total Goals* in a football match where the spread was 2.4 - 2.7 for £100 per goal we could say that the ërealí sell point (if there wasnít a margin built into the quote) should be 2.55, halfway between the sell price of 2.4 and the buy price of 2.7.

Theoretically speaking, the moment you place the trade you are ëlosingí £15. So long as there is a roughly equal number of buyers and sellers at this level, the spread company isnít particularly worried what the make-up is - they know that each client has effectively contributed £15 to their coffers.

Thatís the gloomy news. Of course if an account holder has a winning overall performance then things get rosy very quickly. An individual who has a fractional odds performance of 105%, (he wins 5% more than he loses), tries his hand at Spread Betting. By maintaining a profit of 5% he has not only beaten the margin of approximately 15% built into the bookmakers odds but has possibly been paying 9% tax on all his stakes as well. If he continues his fine performance on the spreads he is liable to end up winning an average of a few points of his stake on every trade. At stake levels of £100 per point this is rapidly going to turn into a commanding advantage over the spread firm. The most successful account holders are earning sums in excess of £100,000 per year; money which is effectively coming out of the pockets of losing clients. To achieve this sort of success with high street or on-course bookmakers would necessitate placing cash bets of approaching £2 million.

Spread Betting firms are generally a lot more tolerant of winning accounts than your high street bookmaker. Bookmakers refuse bets of winning clients when they have been in profit for more than six months or so. The spread companies need to keep markets liquid and turnover high so that they can balance their books and maintain a margin. Some high staking punters also tend to provide a valuable service by offsetting liabilities that have been sustained by a lot of smaller stake trading in one direction; if the England football team make it to the World Cup finals one would guess that a lot of small patriotic money would be supporting England. In reaction to the quotes on England rising, some larger ëprofessionalí investors will at some point be tempted to back against England reasoning that their price is at a higher level than the teams genuine chances.

There is further good news for spread bettors on comparison to their standard betting friends. You would imagine that it would be a straight case of the winners (those who over time win more than their stake) winning a lot more when they turn their hand to Spread Betting, and the losers taking a fast road to the poorhouse. The winners do indeed sprint ahead, but the position for those who lose consistently isnít too gloomy as in Spread Betting there is no such thing as accumulation bets. You cannot tie in one trade to another, so the margin (the difference between the sell price and the buy price) remains roughly the same for all bets. Robbed of the opportunity to lose large amounts on accumulation bets the (losing) newcomer to the world of spreads may actually be ëbetter offí by switching.

Very long losing runs *should* become a thing of the past when taking up Spread Betting. On markets based on performance variables the spread represents the final make-up expected by the traders. By going either side of it you must have at least 45% chance of getting it right on each occasion. Contrast this to the betting shop regular who dutifully places a £10 single on a 6/1 chance. His general expectation of winning must be less than one in six occasions as compared to our spread punter who should pick up at least 45% of the time, even though in the long term he is out of pocket.

You should note that the margin, which effectively represents the spread firms profit on the trade, is not necessarily the same on all markets and even on the same market may be different for buyers and sellers. To illustrate this I found the following example of the *Super Seven/who will score the most goals?* on a Saturday afternoon of Nationwide divisions football:

Wigan	14-17
Notts. Forest	12-15
Man. City	11-14
Middlesborough	11-14
Peterborough	11-14
Watford	9-12
Oldham	8-11

Win = 50 points
Second = 25 points
Third = 10 points
Others = 0 points
Only these seven count.

This is an ëartificialí index in which the total number of points awarded is fixed at 85 (50 + 25 + 10). If, for example, Wigan score four goals, Man.City score three, Watford two, and all the others score one, the points will be assigned Wigan = 50, Man.City = 25, Watford = 10 and others = 0. What would have happened if you simply bought every team? (similar to backing every horse in a race). Adding up the seven ëbuyí figures effectively shows your total expenditure on the bet, 97 points (17 + 15 + 14 + 14 + 14 + 12 + 11). If the results were as above the result of your seven bets would be as follows:

Wigan	buy at 17 m/u 50	win = 33 points
Notts. Forest	buy at 15 m/u 0	lose = 15 points
Man City	buy at 14 m/u 25	win = 11 points
Middlesborough	buy at 14 m/u 0	lose = 14 points
Peterborough	buy at 14 m/u 0	lose = 14 points
Watford	buy at 12 m/u 10	lose = 2 points
Oldham	buy at 11 m/u 0	lose = 11 points
		Total Loss = 12 points

Of course this loss can be simply calculated by subtracting the total ëexpenditureí (97) from the total number of points available (85). Expressed as a simple percentage, in the same way as one might in fractional odds betting, you would be up against more than a 17% margin in favour of the firm. Looking at it in Spread Betting terms, you are losing an average of 1200% of your stake on the series of trades.

The position for sellers is, strangely, considerably better. The sell figures add up to 80 points where 85 are available, so your overall loss of five points represents a margin in favour of the firm of only around 6%. This advantage to sellers appears to go against intuition. Taking another look at the index the ëwiní side of buying looks a far better option than selling. Selling appears to have comparatively few rewards (only up to 14 points win for selling Wigan) but potentially disastrous losses of between 36 and 42 points, depending on the team.

It is in fact the buyers who are struggling against a virtually impossible mountain in the long run. This is far from being an fairly isolated example and it is therefore worth being vigilant of such differential margins on the buy and sell sides.

As a general rule the spread firms are looking for margins in each market of about 10%. Looking at any individual market, the margin should represent around 10% of the possible outcomes. If the spread represents much more than 10% of the possible make-ups then the margin in favour of the spread firms is large, less than 10% and it is on the low side.

On a fixed points index it is comparatively easy to work out the margin as the total number of points available was fixed. On markets based on ëgenuineí sporting variables like the number of goals or runs scored there are no obvious limits. A typical quote on *Total Goals* in a football match might be 2.4 - 2.7, a 0.3 margin. It is clear that the minimum make-up of goals is zero but what about the upper limit? Around 90% of Premiership games produce four or less goals. So 0.3 of four represents a 7.5% margin. But with a small minority of scores falling outside this range the margin might appear to be smaller still. In reality the vast majority of games contain between one and three goals, clustering around the quote. So 0.3 of the difference between one and three is a less generous looking 15%. In top quality competitive events the firms tend to limit their margins, though obscure events which are not liable to attract any serious money are generally subject to higher margins.

As events progress, the difference between the buy and sell figures should decrease. In cricket the margin in Test matches is generally 20 runs at the beginning of an innings. This is supposed to represent approximately 10% of the range of possible make-up values. If the spread on the West Indies starts at 300-320 then we can say that then the 20 point difference in the prices ëtakes outí 10% of the possible make-up values (ranging from 200 - 400) It is quite possible that the final make-up will be outside these two extremes, though in general a +/- figure of 100 would catch the vast majority of possible make-ups.

Should the West Indies be near to completing their innings at 295 /9 with a ërabbití of a batsmen with an average of two facing strike, the possible range of make-up values has drastically diminished. Now we can probably say that the range is somewhere between 295 and 305 for the innings total. The spread should reflect this - in other words the difference between the buy and sell price should perhaps only be one. However this is rarely the case towards the end of a market in running. In the above example it may be three or even five, the latter of which gives a horrendous looking theoretical profit to the spread companies of 50% on bets taken at this stage.

The Importance of Good Prices

Getting a favourable price is all important for long term success. Many serious about their Spread Betting will open accounts with all the firms and pick and choose prices between them. **The difference between taking a 'good' price and a 'poor' one, over time, is critical.** Imagine you are keen on football betting and have one account. You have 100 bets over the course of the season which, for the purposes of this example, happen to all be the same:

> Sell total goals @ 2.4 for £50 per goal

In 63 matches you are correct. In these matches the make-up is two goals. On these 63 occasions you win 0.4 x your £50 stake = £1260 win

In 37 matches you are not correct. In these matches the make-up is three goals. On these 37 occasions you lose 0.6 x your £50 stake = £1110 lose.

Total Profit = £150

This represents a profit of 13%, not at all bad. But letís see what happens if, in just one third of the occasions, our punter had taken a better price from another firm. This better price we will make just 0.1 of a goal more favourable from our example above. Now the record will look like this:

> Sell total goals @ 2.4 for £50 per goal (x 67 bets)
> and
> Sell total goals @ 2.5 for £50 per goal (x33 bets)

In 63 matches you are correct. The make-up is two goals. One third of these (21) matches were sells at 2.5 giving a profit of £525. The other two thirds (42) were sells at 2.4 giving a profit of £840. Total wins = £1365 win.

In 37 matches you are not correct. The make-up is three goals. One third of these (12) matches were sells at 2.5 giving a loss of £300. The other two thirds (25) were sells at 2.4 giving a loss of £750. Total losses = £1050.

Total Profit = £315

The profit has more than doubled by taking what appear to be only slightly better prices. The modest seeming 0.1 of a goal in one third of the games bet on has increased profits by an amazing 110%.

Keeping records of trades is essential not only so that account statements are reconciled, but also as a valuable analysis tool. I recently reviewed my progress according to which sport the bets were placed on and found, much to my surprise, that my cricket trades accounted for over 70% of profits even though I considered football to be my main money spinner. **If you operate what could be loosely termed 'systems' (for example, consistently buying winning distances in**

racing in bad weather), it is very important that you keep track of them in isolation to the rest of you bets. If you have a number of open positions on long term markets the current profit/loss situation should be noted at regular intervals according to the price at which you could close currently.

Knowing the extent of the downside of an individual bet is important. This seems obvious but it is a common mistake that account holders tend to overestimate the potential profit of a trade whilst underestimating the extent to which it can all go wrong. If considering selling the time of the first goal in a football match at 37 for £5 it is easy to imagine the possibility of a goal within the first 10 minutes but when it comes to looking at the downside a voice says, ìdonít worry, in a one sided game like this there is bound to be a goal before longî.

Quantify the downside exactly and be aware of the total potential financial loss, not just that it will be in the region of ëa few points.í In this case it is quite conceivable that the make-up will be 90 if the match is goalless. This means a loss of 53 points totalling £265. It is essential to have this figure at the back of your mind so you can truly assess the potential and staking level of a bet.

As a general rule, in assessing liability, I consider the variability of results using a formula of those that ë*could be reasonably expected on 95% of occasions*í.

For the above example it is fairly easy to calculate that the chances of a 0-0 draw in a football game is around 12%. In this case I would not consider a make-up of 90 as a ëfreakí but a real possibility which must be considered.

Often it is harder to assess the range of possible results. Experience tells me that the ëconceivableí range of winning distances in flat race meeting is 4 to 20 lengths, though on perhaps 5% of occasions the eventual make-ups will fall outside these two extremes. In heavily geared markets a correct assessment is particularly vital. If you are selling the total number of Test match runs in a series what sort of make-up is conceivable if half the playing days are washed out by rain? Here we could be talking of thousands of points.

4 Market Focus: Football

The outstanding feature of this type of theory is that few other people would consider using it.

Betting on football is the core of the spread companiesí business, accounting for up to half of all spread bets placed. They are reliant on widespread TV coverage to generate interest; most of us can remember the times when live matches on TV were limited to FA Cup finals and major international competitions. Channel 5ís coverage of European matches further increases the vast number of games now televised live, and for subscribers to ëSkyí there are weeks when they need only survive one day, strangely Saturday, with no live football on TV. This is a fairly demanding schedule for the betting enthusiast, and as the spread companies are keen to keep clients betting regularly and on as many markets as possible, it is a challenge not to fall into the habit of gambling indiscriminately.

Televised matches offer an embarrassment of riches to the armchair punter. With up to 10 markets updated in running it is easy to feel left out by not having a bet. A usual scenario is having found oneself unable to disagree with the standard quotes on *Goal Supremacy* there then follows a desperate scan of the Corners market or that of ëHow many times will the trainer come on?í in order to have an interest. Readers with accounts will probably recognise this syndrome. And if the individual games arenít enough to send you running to the phone to strike a trade there are always the player performance indices, the total season points indices, relegation, promotion, disciplinary, groups of games supremacy and tournament indices.

Every Premiership match of the season is priced up with a quote on overall ëGoals Supremacyí and a ëTotal Goalsí market. This has a considerable advantage over fixed odds betting where singles are not permitted unless the game is televised live on TV. There is, however, only limited coverage of games in lower divisions and if you happen to live in Scotland, (where football betting makes up a larger proportion of gambling turnover than anywhere else in the UK), you are likely to be sorely disappointed at the lack of coverage.

Goals Supremacy

Through the myriad of bets available the *Goals Supremacy* quote is the staple market on all featured matches. The supremacy spread is the spread firms equivalent of the fixed odds prices and as such becomes the starting point for all calculations. As such, it is usually the market which sees the most serious money. It is expressed in tenths of a goal with the favourite team always listed first irrespective of which team is playing at home. On the occasions that the home team is not favourite it is listed second and the letter ëhí appears next to the team name to denote that they are playing at home.

Taking a fictitious match between Newcastle (playing at home) and Coventry - the spread on the game might be displayed as:

> Newcastle/Coventry 0.5 - 0.8

The fact that there is no such thing as a tenth of a goal in football always stumps the newcomer to Spread Betting. However, imagining your stake as being expressed also in tenths makes it a little more clear. If you buying at 0.8 in this example at £100 per goal you are effectively betting one tenth of your stake (£10) per tenth of a goal. If Newcastle win with a one goal supremacy (1-0; 2-1; 3-2 etc.) you win the difference between 0.8 and 1= 0.2 (£20).

A two goal victory sees you winning the difference between 0.8 and 2 = 1.2 (£120). a draw results in a supremacy make-up of 0, so as a buyer you would lose the difference between 0.8 and 0 (£80). We could view the above example as a ëtypicalí match in terms of the expected supremacy of the home team. In all UK football, for teams playing others in the same division, there are baseline figures for the relative frequencies of home victories/away victories and draws.

Percentage of home victories	49%
Percentage of matches drawn	26%
Percentage of away victories	25%

These are the figures over which all other information about the teamsí abilities must be placed. The extent to which home advantage is a factor appears extraordinary. Almost twice as many home sides achieve a win compared to those playing away. If, in our example, Coventry were the home team it is likely that it would be they, not Newcastle, that are given a supremacy rating. There is one particular exception to this rule; local derbies tend to be virtually evenly matched in terms of general home/away supremacy.

The percentage likelihood of a match ending in a draw is fairly consistent. The chances of a draw are decreased to a lower limit of about 22% when one team is judged to have an overwhelming superiority, and can increase to around 32% when there are likely to be very few goals scored. Drapkin and Forsyth, authors of ë*The Punters Revenge*í conclusively showed it is a fallacy to assume that draws tend to happen mostly between teams of equal ability.

This seems remarkable but it is the case that, in general, draws happen as frequently in matches where one team is seen as superior as they do for teams whose chances are closely matched; i.e. Arsenal v Manchester Utd. has essentially the same chance of being a draw as Arsenal v Southampton despite the fact that Arsenal would be fancied (in terms of their expected supremacy) much more heavily to beat the latter. The implication of this is that the good old British pastime of filling in a pools coupon every week is essentially a chance gamble and not subject to any significant degree of skill.

Going back to the original example of the Newcastle v Coventry match; if we were to look at the fixed odds on offer on this match they would probably look like this:

Newcastle (home)	10/11	(52.4%)
Coventry (away)	11/4	(26.7%)
Draw	9/4	(30.8%)

The percentage is the equivalent for the odds on offer.(See Appendix for explanation of odds/percentages.) These figures include the book-makers overound of 10% so if you were to deduct 10% from each figure (52.4% minus 10% becomes 47.2%, etc.) you get very close to the general percentages for home and away teams performance presented above.

On a coupon for a normal Saturday of league fixtures you might come across around a third of matches priced up at this sort of level. Some home teams will be rated far more highly, others less so. However the fact that this is a fairly typical match allows us to take a general view of the spread. It should be borne in mind that even though Newcastle are awarded a ëhead startí on the supremacy quote of more than half a goal this does not mean that the most likely result is a Newcastle win. In fact it is more likely that Newcastle wonít win.

Looking back at the general frequency table you can see that the chances of the match resulting in Newcastle failing to win are 25% (the chance of an away victory) plus 26% (the chance of a draw), totalling 51%. If we accept that the chances of a Newcastle win are only 49% then buying them at 0.8 suddenly doesnít look particularly attractive. On these figures there is a more than 50% chance that buyers will lose at least 0.8 of a goal.

This seems to go against intuition. If you were to glance at the above quote it would be easy to come to the conclusion that the most likely result would be a Newcastle win by one goal. To demonstrate that this would be a misreading of the spread I examined a sample of 400 league matches where the supremacy spread was 0.5 - 0.8 in favour of the home team.

Actual supremacy of teams playing at home with supremacy rating of 0.5 - 0.8

7 goals	6 goals	5 goals	4 goals	3 goals	2 goals
0.5%	0.5%	0.5%	2.2%	6.0%	15.3%

1 goal	0 goals	- 1 goals	-2 goals	-3 goals
23.1%	27.1%	17.0%	5.9%	1.7%

In my sample 48.1% of home teams won, 27.1% were draws and 24.6% ended in away wins; a reasonably representative sample of all league games. The figures confirm that a draw (0 goals supremacy) is a more likely result than a one goal win to the home team. As a buyer at 0.8 you would win on every result to the left of nil goals supremacy. Indiscriminately buying teams with a supremacy of 0.8 would result in wins on 48% of occasions. On almost half of the winning trades you would gain a rather measly 0.2 of a goal (for the times when there was a supremacy of one goal).

The saving grace is the comparatively few occasions when the home team wins by two goals or more; though remember there is generally a maximum make-up imposed of five goals supremacy which would stunt the wins considerably when your favoured team goes goal crazy. The seller at 0.5 wins on more occasions; all the results to the right of one goal supremacy, a total of over 51% of the time. However the number of really juicy wins that can be looked forward to is small in comparison with the buyer.

On these figures buyers would lose £75 for every £50 won whereas sellers losses would be smaller at £56 for every £50 won. So it could be said that buying supremacy as a general tactic has very little going for it. This position is mirrored in fixed odds betting where the quickest way to the poorhouse is to indiscriminately back odds on teams in the 2/5 to 8/11 region. The vast weight of football backersí money goes on short priced teams. Most of this is frittered away on vast accumulative bets on five or more selections, despite the efforts of the serious betting press to dissuade punters from this course.

This is almost the reverse of the situation in racing where it is the longer priced selections that generally have a greater profit margin for the bookmaker built in. Here the betting shop fraternity tend to try and find winners at longer prices even though there is a weight of evidence to suggest that, in general, runners at long prices represent appalling value. When it comes to filling in their football coupons they become hell bent on backing odds on favourites, falling foul of the greater profit margins the bookmaker picks up on short priced teams.

I have little doubt that in general the supremacy of teams tends to be overestimated by the footballing public and indeed most newspaper tipsters. A good way to demonstrate this is to look at the forecasts of tipsters from national newspapers. Taking a selection of ëtypicalí matches where the home team would be awarded a supremacy of 0.5 - 0.8 (a fixed odds price of narrowly odds on), the newspaper tipsters produced the following selections: (The ëcorrectí frequencies are in brackets).

Home team to win	77.5%	(49%)
Away team to win	7.5%	(26%)
Draw	15.0 %	(25%)

The predicted frequency of home wins is astonishingly high, made up for by the implied assertion that draws and away wins happen very rarely. You canít really blame them. If asked to chose between three possible alternatives where one (the home win) has around a 50% of turning up it would be sticking your neck out to choose one of the other alternatives.

In our example of Newcastle versus Coventry, lets assume the form book, league table positions, or whatever facts we chose to base our estimate of the games result on, all appear to point to a home win. In all honesty if we were to come up with our own assessment of the home sides supremacy I feel that most of us would tend to pitch it somewhere between one and two goals. The TV pundits tend to reinforce this view. A game where the home team seem to be marginally superior will probably be forecast to be 1-0 or 2-1 ahead by the end of 90 minutes. Where the gap in form is a bit wider they might plump for 2-0. England against an obscure East European nation? Must be 3-0.

In forecasting results it is all too easy to fall into a predetermined way of thinking about the likely advantage the ëbetterí team has, and on most occasions our intuitive assessments will overestimate the chances of the favourites.

It can be useful to draw up comparisons between the fixed odds offered for teams (available on coupons from the chains of bookmakers) and their spread equivalents. To do this requires comparing two totally different betting systems, but it is a useful exercise as it routinely highlights examples of where the fixed odds companies and the spreads are disagreeing. The following is my estimate of supremacy ratings related to fixed odds. There has to be some margin for error here as there are five companies regularly offering fixed odds quotes on all professional matches and another four spread companies.

The figures also donít take into account the slightly differing draw prices that are offered. For example, top international matches are drawn on slightly more occasions than British league matches. In cases where the draw price would be lower the supremacy rating may also be slightly lower.

Supremacy	Fixed odds price for favourites	Fixed odds price for non-favourites
0.15yc	6/4	6/4
0 - 0.3	5/4	7/4
0.1 - 0.4	6/5	15/8
0.2 - 0.5	11/10	2/1
0.3 - 0.6	evs	9/4
0.4 - 0.7	10/11	5/2
0.5 - 0.8	4/5	3/1
0.6 - 0.9	4/6	7/2
0.7 - 1.0	8/13	4/1
0.8 - 1.1	4/7	9/2
0.9 - 1.2	8/15	5/1
1.0 - 1.3	1/2	11/2
1.1 - 1.4	4/9	6/1
1.2 - 1.5	2/5	13/2
1.3 - 1.6	4/11	7/1
1.4 - 1.7	1/3	15/2
1.5 - 1.8	3/10	8/1
1.6 - 1.9	2/7	17/2
1.7 - 2.0	1/4	9/1

To have an estimated supremacy of one goal the favoured team must be very heavily odds on. A supremacy rating of around two is virtually unheard of in Premiership matches. Although I refer to ëfixedí odds the bookmakers are discouraging the use of this term as they reserve the right to change them, though in practice the odds you see on the printed coupons will be the odds you get. Comparing the two types of betting can provide some interesting comparisons and is liable to throw up some excellent fixed odds bets as well as being a pointer to which way the spread markets are moving.

Occasionally the two types of odds go significantly out of line. Where the favourites are rated at 4/5 there are regularly spreads of 0.3 - 0.6 supremacy whereas the ëcorrectí quote should be 0.5 - 0.8. In a recent Premiership match between Barnsley and Blackburn there was a particularly large price difference. Barnsley, playing at home had suffered some heavy defeats and were 11/4 with Ladbrokes as opposed to the quote of 4/5 for Blackburn. This would suggest a supremacy rating of 0.5 - 0.8 for Blackburn with the spread companies; in fact the spread stood at 1.0-1.3. If you received quotes of that magnitude for all teams rated at 4/5 you would be able to sell consistently and watch the money roll in. (The result of the Barnsley match was a draw).

It might be that you suspect it is the spread companies who get it right consistently and value is to be had on the fixed odds coupon. If you see the spread on a particular game start moving significantly, as they often do with live games, then the immovable fixed odds price is effectively left in the starting blocks. If you essentially agree with the assessment of the new spread quotes then there must be a good price to be had from the fixed odds companies.

Any hopes of being able to arbitrage fixed odds prices and spread quotes are unfounded. It is practically impossible because the supremacy of a team is essentially open ended. If you wish to demonstrate this yourself take a deliberately extreme example; for instance if Liverpool were to be offered at 3/1 to win at Spurs but also have a spread supremacy rating of one - you will still find it a hopeless task to juggle the stakes about in such a way as to make a profit from all possible outcomes.

If are looking to wager on the actual result of a game then the *Goal Supremacy* market should be your first point of reference. However the fact that the gearing is so low on this market can often make it look somewhat unappealing whether as a buyer and a seller. In an ëaverageí game where the supremacy is set at 0.5 - 0.8 the superiority of the favourites usually appears quite clear on paper. Assuming that the favourites are at home, they will almost certainly have a better record playing at home than their opponents away from home. You may be able to find encouraging signs in the away teams recent performances but you may have to dig rather deeply to find realistic reasons why they might be able to pull off an unexpected away victory.

The seller knows that the trading point of 0.5 means that the reward for the match being drawn is equivalent to the loss for the match being won by the favourites by a single goal: not a particularly enticing situation since it might appear that a victory for the favourites is slightly more likely. As a buyer the situation looks even less exiting. The most likely looking result, a victory by the home team by one goal, yields a derisory looking profit of 0.2 with a downside of four times that figure if the favourites fail to win. It is only when the home teams wins by a clear two goals or more that the profit looks more healthy. In games of this sort it is quite difficult to see beyond a make-up of more than +/- 1 goal which has the effect of making the margin between the quotes of 0.3 appear huge.

The situation where the quote straddles a whole goal is particularly strange. If a team is quoted with a 0.9 - 1.2 supremacy rating buyers only win when the favourites win by two clear goals; sellers win only if the match ends in a draw or shock victory for the underdogs.

Total goals

The other major market on football is the quote on the *Total Goals* scored by both teams in a match. I suspect that the total goals market may be more popular than that of team supremacy. It is particularly enticing for viewers of live TV matches. Here, those wishing to have a speculative bet without having to predict the actual result are drawn to buying the total goals index hoping for an action packed goal feast. Traders have gone on record as confirming that this is the case.

One of the worst individual matches from the spread companies point of view was when Blackburn beat Sheffield Wednesday 7-2 in a match televised by Sky early in the 1997/98 season; one of a clump of live matches at the time where goals werenít hard to come by. The companiesí losses on this match demonstrate the scarcity of total goal sellers to balance their books, though I would suggest that any profits accrued from buying goals around this time would be eaten away fairly quickly, as the theory behind the tactic (seemingly to add a bit of excitement for the disinterested) must rank fairly low down on the all time roll call of gambling systems.

I would hesitate to call any Spread Betting market ëeasy to readí but my researches into *Total Goals* suggest that the number of goals in a single match does bear a strong relationship to the teamsí previous results and, as such, profits can be made if effort is put into analysing the factors that contribute to high (or low) scoring matches.

In Premiership matches in the most recently completed season, home teams scored an average of 1.47 goals per game. Away teams managed an average of 1.08 goals per game. Subtract one from the other and you come out with 0.39 supremacy in favour of the home teams. The average across matches in all competitions is nearer 0.5 demonstrating that the Premiership has, in general, slightly fewer goals than an ëaverageí football match. A standard quote for a total goals in a Premiership match would be 2.4 - 2.7. The figures above for home team goals per game (1.47) added to those for away teams (1.08) give us an expected frequency of 2.55 goals per Premiership game. This, not surprisingly, falls neatly between the buy and sell figure of the most usual quote. Quotes tend not to fall below this level very far. You may see quotes of 2.2 - 2.5 for drab looking internationals and European games; (in particular Manchester United are gaining something of a reputation for ëlookingí for a 0-0 draw in their European away games.) Italian Serie A matches (covered on Channel 4) have less goals per game than the English Premiership.

As one teamís superiority rating increases then the *Total Goals* quote goes up accordingly as it is expected that the strong favourites have a chance of giving the underdogs a thrashing. Hence, when the teams supremacy is quoted at around the 1.4 - 1.7 mark (here the favourites are deemed to be very strong), the total goals quote will increase slightly to 2.6 - 2.9.

Looking in general at the relative fortunes of buyers and sellers of *Total Goals*, a theme which we see in many markets reoccurs; sellers win more often than buyers but the buyers can look forward to a few larger payouts when the goals tally goes through the roof. Assuming that the spread is set at 2.4 - 2.7 a seller has a maximum win of 2.4 points. In Premiership games 1996-1997 just over 6% of games produced six or more goals, yielding profits for the buyer of at least 3.3 points. The most likely score that either team will achieve is one (for both home and away teams) and therefore the most likely number of goals in a game is two. This total of two accounted for 27% of all Premiership games. If you add on the number of times that a game finished goal-less or with just one goal then this percentage rises to 54%, a clear majority of games.

For most Premiership games buyers will only start winning when goal or more goals are scored- this only happens in 46% of games. Having been disparaging of those who buy goals in search of excitement it has to be said that selling them in a live game does not exactly add up to a enjoyable eveningsí entertainment as oneís nerves start jangling whenever the ball goes near either penalty area.

Mark Pullein, writing in the *Racing and Football Outlook* has put forward an interesting set of rules for predicting 0-0 draws for fixed odds betting purposes and the ideas presented here follow on from his work on the subject, adapted for Spread Betting markets.

The most logical way of trying to predict how many goals will be scored in a game would appear to be to look at how many the teams in question scored in previous games. Presumably, anyone taking a cursory glance at the teamsí records would tend to base their predictions on this strategy, however Pullein suggests a technique with greater predictive value that involves examining the goal scoring record of the home teamsí attack in conjunction with the away teamsí record of conceding goals. We know that the average number of goals scored by the home team is 1.47 per game. It therefore follows that the away sides are letting in 1.47 goals per game.

If you find a game in which a home team with a poor attack (scoring less than 1.47 goals per game) plays a team with a good defensive record (conceding less than 1.47 goals away from home) then a low scoring game is indicated.

To put this to the test I concentrated on the recent form - the last games for each team. I looked at 500 league games from all divisions where I had details of the recent form of each team prior to the game. Of the 500 games, 25 featured teams which had a home average of less than 0.75 goals playing a team which had conceded less than 0.75 goals on their travels. Here the averages were at their lowest and if the theory was to work at all it should do in these cases.

The results were fairly remarkable; an average of just two goals per game and a large theoretical profit had one been able to sell. *Total Goals* on these occasions. When the criteria were loosened and I considered games where the home team was scoring less than one goal per home game, and the opposition conceding less than 1 goal per away game, the resulting matches produced an average of 2.3 goals per game (slightly lower than the bottom end of the majority of quotes on *Total Goals*).

The outstanding feature of this type of theory is that few other people would consider using it. It is all to easy to conclude that two high scoring teams produce games with higher goals than the average and two low scoring teams produce fewer goals. Here the logic is refined to come up with a theory that potentially has great predictive value yet is largely unnoticed - the perfect combination of characteristics for spread enthusiasts.

Team Performance

Though they are the cornerstone of football spreads, many account holders must be tempted to overlook the overall *Goal Supremacy* market as there are only a very limited number of potential make-ups. Perhaps due to this inherent lack of appeal all the companies are now offering *Team Performance* spreads for live games.

Of all the spread markets these are possibly my favourites as you can wager on them to reflect any number of possible characteristics that a game might take on. For all major games a Performance quote on both teams is offered. Quotes are made on the basis of awarding points to (and deducting points from) both teams, depending on various performance criteria. There is an irritation in that the four UK spread companies all have varying criteria. At the time of writing they were:

Hills
Win = 25
Draw = 10
Goal = 20
Corner = 5
Yellow Card = -5
Red Card = -15

Sporting Index
Win = 25
Draw = 10
Goal = 15
Corner = 3
Yellow card = -5
Red card = - 15
Hit Woodwork = 10
(rebounds into play)

IG Index
Goal = 25
Corner = 3
Goal conceded = -10
Yellow card = -10
Red card = -25
1 point per minute that team keeps clean sheet

City Index
Win = 30
Draw = 10
Goal = 15
first goal = 10
Clean Sheet = 15
Corner = 3

Although these values may have changed by now, they can serve as an illustration as to how the differences might affect your strategy.

The difference in the way that the markets are calculated is such that there is nothing to be gained in comparing quotes on the same match. In many respects this is a deliberate ploy by the spread firms so that account holders are unable to ëshop aroundí for the best prices. Taking the best prices on offer leads to a lack of two-way trading (roughly equal proportions of buyers and sellers for each market), leading to a cut in the spread firmís profit margins. This, of course, is the best reason in the world why account holders should try to get the best price available even if it means the arduous task of comparing prices where the markets are calculated differently.

Since the gearing is heavy on the Performance markets it is possible to see which way the money is going on a particular match by noting the change in prices up to kick off. It is not unusual to see swift changes in the indices as money comes on. These changes are not so evident on the less heavily geared *Goals Supremacy* market.

Each set of scoring criteria place slightly different emphasis on the factors. Ideally the weighting of points should reflect the relative chances of a particular event happening. It would clearly be wrong to award a corner 10 points if a goal was awarded only 20, as corners would have too much importance relative to goals. Recently Hills have changed their scoring structure, awarding 25 points for a win. This leaves only IG index as the sole company not to award a substantial bonus for actually winning the match, which, after all, is what the game is about. IG are particularly hot on discipline; with 25 points subtracted for a red card. The following table is a ëready reckonerí of expected make-ups with the five companiesí performance indexes. This necessitates the use of a lot of ëaveragesí for yellow cards and corners but broadly reflects how actual scores should translate into make-ups.

Estimated make-ups for each match score on the spread companies performance indices

Match score	Sporting Index	Hills	IG Index	City Index
0 - 0	28 - 28	53 - 53	88 - 88	40-40
1 - 1	33-33	73 - 73	50 - 50	45 -45
2 - 2	48 -48	93 - 93	65 -65	60 - 60
1 - 0	61 -6	88 - 43	116 - 22	76 -12
2 - 1	66 - 20	108 - 63	88 - 37	85 - 30
2 - 0	80 - 2	108 - 43	143 - 10	106 - 12
3 - 2	86 - 33	130 - 81	86 - 35	103 - 43
3 - 1	86 - 17	131 - 61	102 - 4	104 - 27
3 - 0	98 - -3	132 - 41	177 - -25	125 - 6
4 - 0	114 - -2	150 - 40	202 - -35	140 - 6

IGís awarding of a point for each minute a team keeps a clean sheet is particularly innovative and ensures that it gives their index considerable volatility. Hills recent revamp of their performance indices ensures that their volatility is also high . The stated figures for IG in particular should be read with caution; a team that loses 1 - 0 to an injury time goal is going to be 89 points better off than a team losing 1 - 0 to a goal scored in the first minute.

One should be wary of the consequences of the referee handing out lots of cards. In Italian and Spanish games (frequently shown live on Channel 4 and Sky respectively) the average number of cards per game is virtually double that of British matches. The net effect is that the performance quotes of both teams will be lower than an equivalent game in Britain as there are liable to be a greater proportion of points knocked off both teams for disciplinary offences.

Having made your decision on which team you are favouring you are faced with two choices of bet. You can either buy your favoured team or sell your unfancied team. This decision largely rests on your reading of how many goals there are likely to be. If you tend towards a low scoring game then you are liable to be at an advantage selling the team you are backing against, or buying your favoured team if you predict an open game with plenty of goals. I was faced with a similar conundrum recently when attempting to back Stoke in an end of season First Division game with Manchester City. The previous dayís Premiership matches (on the critical second-to-last weekend of the season) had produced the largest number of goals of the entire season.

I confidently expected that the weekendsí trend would continue for the Stoke v Manchester City match which would decide which club would be relegated. Expecting Stoke to win a high scoring game I bought them on a Performance Index. Stoke lost 5-2 and were relegated, the sort of result that should in no way have rewarded me with a win of any kind. In fact I ended up with a small win as Stokes two goals ensured enough points to make-up higher than their Performance quote, despite the fact they were comprehensively beaten.

If you wish to oppose a team that are the clear favourites then my suggestion would be to sell them rather than buying the opposition. In my experience teams that fail to assert their expected superiority produce a greater profit on their sell side than the profit from buying the underdogs. This is due to the fact that, in general, underdogs perform well by frustrating the opposition into a low scoring match. The lower the number of goals the less points there are to be assigned, hence the less chance of the favourites achieving their expected high Performance rating.

It should be noted that the Performance Indices cannot be traded in running. There is only a single update at half time when it is possible to trade. You may be able to effectively ëcloseí a performance bet by taking out an opposite trade on the overall *Goal Supremacy* market. If you bought one of the teams on the Performance Index and are looking at a substantial profit with just 20 minutes to go, it may be possible to lock in an overall profit by selling the *Goal Supremacy* of the team you had initially backed. This requires some quick mental arithmetic but is a valid option if you feel the last phase of a game might be going against you.

Subsidiary Markets

The two subsidiary factors that make up the Performance Indexes, those relating to the *Yellow/Red Cards* given to a team and the *Numbers Of Corners Won*, can also be wagered on separately. Unlike the Performance Indices however, one can only bet on the match totals, not the individual team totals.

Looking at the English Premiership the number of corners a team wins is related to its goal scoring and winning capabilities, though the difference between the best and the worst teams is, surprisingly, not that great. Premiership champions of 1996/1997, Manchester Utd. averaged 6.9 corners per home game, whilst conceding 4.2, but their superiority in terms of goals was 38 - 17. If corners won were a direct reflection of goals scored you would expect the gap between the corners won and those conceded to be somewhat greater. (If they were exactly proportional you would expect Man. Utd. to win 7.7 and concede just 3.4 per home game).

At the other end of the scale Nottingham Forestís away record contributed to them finishing bottom of the league. Their corners record in away games was an average of 4.4 won and 6.6 conceded but their goal record was proportionally a lot worse, scoring 16 goals in the season and conceding 32. (Again, if their corners record was exactly proportional to their goals record you would expect them to have won 3.7 corners and conceded 7.3 per away game). The lesson out of all this is that corners partially reflect a teams superiority though perhaps not as starkly as one might imagine. It would be easy to assume that ëgoodí teams hammered ëpoorí teams when it comes to the corners tally; in fact this really is not the case.

In the Premiership, clubs playing at home win 6.2 corners and concede 4.6 on average, hence quotes on corners tend to be around the 11-12 mark. The 1996/97 top (home) corner winners were Liverpool (8.2), Newcastle (7.5) and Wimbledon (7.0). Iím not convinced that the corners market on its own is anything more than a bit of a thrill to help live matches along. There is a theory that the number of corners that a game produces is dependent in some way on the size of the pitch though I have to confess Iím not inclined to look into this in much detail. **The frequency of corners throughout matches is volatile - like buses they tend to come in three's.** It is said that the client with the worst financial losses in the short history of Spread Betting was a consistent buyer of the corners market. I hope the gentlemen concerned at least got plenty of excitement out of his wagers as I am rather at a loss as to what his overall strategy must have been.

For a truly bizarre football viewing experience, try selling the *Bookings Index*. This is available on all live games and is scored as 10 points for a yellow card, 25 for a red. As a seller you find yourself flinching every time players from opposing sides get within five yards of one another and remonstrating with the referee to be more lenient on what you see as harmless tackles.

Being of a peace-loving disposition I have never bought the *Bookings Index* but I dare say it must lead to a good deal of fist waving as the buyer exhorts the participants into life threatening challenges.

The bookings index clearly revolves around the disciplinary records of the players involved and the record of the official in charge of the match. *The Racing Post* gives an excellent guide as to the current relevant stats. The most striking thing about referees is their general inconsistency when it comes to handing out cards. By assigning points in the same way as the spread companies it turns out that the most lenient referee in a season hands out roughly half the number of ëpointsí as he who is most strict.

Arriving at a ëcorrectí quote is simply a case of overlaying the record of the referee on the clubs record in the season and as such it is difficult to see where the astute backer could hope to be in possession of knowledge that the spread companies are not aware of. It helps to be aware of some ëbad bloodí between the teams that might set the teams, or indeed the fans, in a vengeful mood - a leading player recently transferred from one side to another for instance.

I know of an account holder who swears by selling the *Bookings Index* on Italian and Spanish games. The starting quote for these matches is around the 55 - 59 mark, significantly higher than the 31-35 more usual for Premiership games. Here the seller can certainly expect to win from a game more times than they lose, the trick is to try and avoid the small number of blood baths which end up in make-ups of 150+.

Players on the ë*Time of the First Goal market*í tend to be dominated by those who sell in the hope of seeing a team with a high overall supremacy get an early goal.

The reasoning behind this is unsound. If the quote on supremacy is, in your opinion, too low then one should buy it or a related *Performance Index*. If you judge it correct then there is no reason to assume that the time of the first goal quote is mysteriously too high. In fact the time of the first goal in all games averages out at around 36 minutes. Teams with high supremacy only score their opening goal fractionally quicker than the average and the spread companies are perfectly capable of adjusting the spread to take this into account.

This raises a general rule about ëtrading on your beliefsí. If you genuinely predict a lot of goals, buy goals; donít try and extend this to other markets and conclude that the game clearly will also be very open, therefore buying corners might be a better bet.

Betting in Running

The ability to trade in running is deservedly hailed as the major leap forward that Spread Betting has introduced. The opportunity to trade whilst the game is going on is facilitated by the captioned display of Teletext prices in the corner of the TV screen. Trading in running is subject to the same principles as any other betting; if you think you know something, get in early before everyone else has the same idea. Trading in running means that the time frames you are working in are seconds.

Four minutes into a game you realise that the away team in a European fixture are playing a lone striker up front and otherwise getting 10 men behind the ball - they have absolutely no aim other than play for a 0-0 draw. In these circumstances the quote of 2.6 - 2.9 total goals in the game looks too high. It is little use to ëwait and see what happensí or for the commentators to start reporting on the defensive tactics - a couple of minutes more and the quote may slump to 2.3 - 2.6. This is the essential nature of trading in running: it doesnít give you any particular advantage or even necessarily the option of ëchanging your mindí as it is sometimes promoted (who honestly can say that theyíve closed a bet for a loss without a goal being scored), it simply means that you have less time to consider your decisions.

During play in a football game the quotes naturally ëdeclineí as the game goes on. If a team starts a game with a supremacy of 1.0 - 1.3 but fails to score in the first 15 minutes their supremacy might be reduced to 0.9 - 1.2. This reflects the fact that one sixth of the game has gone without them ëassertingí their supremacy. Should they continue to fail to score their quote will fall in steady increments every 10 minutes or so. Should they score in the 66th minute when their supremacy quote has fallen to 0.5 - 0.8 then the goal they have scored is added on to their supremacy instantly, so one would expect a revised quote of 1.5 - 1.8.

It is important to understand the way in which the quotes on the market ëebb and flowí; imagine a situation where you have bought total goals at 2.9. In the 60th minute one team goes 3 - 0 up taking you into a guaranteed win position. The quote now stands at 3.9 - 4.1. You are inclined to sell and take your profit of one goal as you feel the winning side may ease off. In this situation you may choose to play a waiting game, albeit a very short one of about four minutes, and hope that your position will improve with another goal being scored. If it doesnít and you time it perfectly you will probably get a ëfreeí couple of good attacks by either side and even if a goal isnít scored be able to still sell at 3.9 a few minutes later. This skill of catching of quotes before they change is useful to refine if you are to profit from trading in running.

Forecasting Strategies

Having described the mechanics of football spreads the only thing left to know is the small matter of predicting the results of matches. Even though they may not be aware of it, most people who bet regularly apply a set of rules to matches they are trying to predict. Forecasting draws for the purpose of the pools has been an enduring hobby for many millions, though its dominance in the nationís gambling psyche is largely been replaced by the national lottery. With the emergence of widespread fixed odds betting and now Spread Betting there is a huge marketplace for football prediction systems and strategies. Having reviewed many of them it is clear that the concept of seeking ëvalueí in betting is still not as widespread as it should be.

One of the largest organisations in the UK to provide football tips is intent on sending its members recommendations to perm ten home forecasts: invariably these ten are simply a selection of the shortest odds on teams playing that week. Although the ëseriousí betting press constantly make the point that value betting is the only way of providing long term profit the message does not seem to get through to the substantial number of punters with their football forms on a Saturday morning. I am not sure that, in general, those with Spread Betting accounts are any more sophisticated in their football betting - published interviews with spread firms traders tend to suggest that their clients biases and mistakes in forecasting are broadly the same as those of their fixed-odds counterparts.

The British 'disease' that afflicts football forecasting is to overestimate the winning potential of the match favourites in any one game. I would estimate that up to 75% of all stakes go on teams who are rated at 4/5 and below. I set about studying the outcome of backing only short priced favourites (teams rated at stronger than 4/5) against backing teams to win at all the higher prices (above 4/5).

% of stake retained (after tax) backing short odds teams	% of stake retained (after tax) backing teams at higher prices
80.0%	85.8%

(sample = 800 British league and Cup games)

Although not a huge difference it is certainly enough to consider seriously. The bookmakers appear to be taking more profit from their short odds enthusiasts than anyone else. There is an important difference between fixed odds football betting and Spread Betting which relates to strike rates. The obvious attraction of betting at short prices on the fixed odds is the high percentage of winners found. Although we have seen that backing teams at longer odds retains slightly more stake, in general the strike rate is low (In my sample there was a theoretical losing run of 20 matches). As stated previously, selling a teamís supremacy results in a slightly higher win ratio than buying supremacy. In addition, this tactic retains more stake money, therefore as a seller of supremacy you are at an advantage on both counts.

Global Performance Supremacy

Punters perception of teams, and indeed the basis on which spread prices are formulated, are largely determined by two factors: the position of the team in league tables and what one could loosely describe as the ëprestigeí rating of a team. **In general, forecasters have a very rigid view of a team's league position.**

A lot of people who predict draws on the pools are quite keen on a system which is based on finding home teams who are placed a number of positions lower than the away team. The superiority of the away team is thus said to counterbalance the advantage of home supremacy - the result; surely a draw. Though most people know that the English league is very volatile (teams at the bottom of league tables are quite capable of overturning leaders) they shy away from betting on such a result and tend to place too much emphasis on the apparently better chances of a team placed higher in the table than their opposition.

ëPrestigeí is also a factor in determining odds. I am convinced that **certain sides are consistently overvalued in the betting markets** and consequently less glamorous outfits are undervalued. From the Premiership certain clubs spring to mind easily. Wimbledon and Derby provide excellent value for money. In the lower divisions there is a general tendency to overvalue the bigger clubs who are experiencing harder times. Wolves, Birmingham and for some reason Burnley fit into this category, even though plenty of fans of the latter canít remember the time they were playing in the top division. It follows that if our goal is making a long term profit, then we need to find value betting opportunities that are based on considerations that others are not using to come to their conclusions.

In my experience the best football betting opportunities arise when current form and league position go ëout of stepí. The most perfect opportunity to ëget a favouriteí is when a team near the top of the league who is out of form plays one near the bottom who is in form. Opportunities for this type of bet appear with surprising frequency. The definition of ëgoodí and ëbadí current form is somewhat subjective. If a home team is given a supremacy of around the 0.5 - 0.8 mark then I would class ëbad formí as not having won a game in their last four. For the away team ëgood formí would generally be noted if they had won two out of their last four matches.

On first studying the facts of teamsí recent performances it is enlightening to see the extent to which top teams go through poor non-winning patches and similarly how lowly placed teams put together a run of matches unbeaten. By using these quite simple criteria I believe it is relatively easy to come out ahead. Unfortunately it is not possible to have a spread bet on all the Football League and Scottish games as one can with fixed odds betting otherwise I would be reasonably confident in my ability at opposing favourites to profit consistently.

The FA Cup is generally seen as the place that favourites fail. Despite its reputation there is no evidence that teams from lower divisions playing more illustrious opposition are undervalued in the betting markets. Though they achieve a small percentage of ëshockí results these are no more than the odds suggest. Teams from lower divisions have quite a poor record in replays - they seem to manage a Herculean effort to draw in the first match but donít generally have the ability to compete as effectively in the replay.

In fact the real place for shocks is the League cup where Premiership teams have lately had a torrid time in matching their supremacy ratings. The competition is losing its prestige for the top teams, to the extent that we have in the last couple of seasons seen Manchester United field ëBí or even ëCí teams in the early ties and seemingly not that bothered when they get eliminated from the competition. The motivation for the other Premiership teams similarly seems to be reduced with the effect that clubs from the lower divisions are in with chances far greater than their odds suggest.

I particularly favour selling a Premiership clubís supremacy when playing a team from the second division. The supremacy spread here tends to stand around the 1.5 - 1.8 mark, (equivalent to odds of about 8/1 for the away team). Yet, put a relatively unmotivated Premier team against a lower division, (who are prepared to throw everything they have at the game), and previous results from the last few years bear out the fact that the top teams superiority is, in fact, very low.

Another general trend to watch for is the fact that teams struggling to avoid relegation tend to do a lot better than their quotes imply towards the end of the season - especially when playing against teams that are mid-table and have little to play for. It is important to look at this phenomena in the eight matches prior to the end of the season and not simply the last couple of fixtures, when quotes on relegation threatened teams tumble in their matches against those with a better placing.

British teams in International competition

Consider these two contradictory views of British teams standing in world football.

The English national team was entered into the ëTournoi de Franceí alongside Brazil, Italy and France in a warm up friendly tournament for the 1998 World Cup. In the British press there was talk of the fact that England shouldnít be competing on the same stage as these illustrious names of World footballing history. By the second game of the three matches England had already won the tournament.

Compare this with the view taken on the top English teams in European competition. Chelsea go to Tromso, Norway with a supremacy estimate of around 1.6 and a string of predictions, not least from the ëSporting Lifeí of a clear three goal victory. Chelsea end up being frozen out in the Arctic conditions and were ëluckyí to lose the match 3-2.

Although it is clearly unreasonable to take examples in isolation, there is a lesson to be learned about the national psyche from these examples that is of tremendous use in Spread Betting. Opinion polls have, incredibly, demonstrated that the English sense of nationality is inextricably bound up with the performance of our football teams. We are all aware of the tendency for the public and press to overreact to football results. A couple of good wins and the England coach is sainted, an embarrassing defeat and they are heaped with public ignominy.

The same **overreaction** is definitely reflected in football betting. In general British teams, (whether it be national or domestic teams), apparently facing a comparatively simple task, have their chances overestimated. Those who appear to face a stiffer challenge tend to have their chances underestimated. The fixed odds on British teams against weaker opposition are pretty unattractive and backing them at these prices consistently would ensure a very expensive long term loss. The spread firms, which are generally in line with the fixed odds firms when trading begins on a game tend to find plenty of buyers for the British *Team Performance.* You can confirm this for yourself by checking the prices for the European competitions on the day of the match. When a match is shown live in the evening this characteristic is particularly visible - there is a marked tendency for the Britsí Performance quote to rise.

As a general rule a British team that starts favourite will strengthen on all the markets. I would be interested to know the motivation of the individuals are who are putting money on British. They may, knowing a live match is on TV get a sudden stirring of patriotism, or they may be being sucked into the aforementioned illusion of overestimating supremacy on a big scale. If you really feel the quote on a British team is good value then the advice must be to take the price early. As a seller of British teams it generally pays to wait until the last moment.

Although it may not be as pronounced, in terms of the betting market, British teams are able to survive admirably when they face tough competition. Iím quite keen on backing British teams on the spreads when they are playing away in Spain or Italy. Whereas we tend to have a condescending attitude to countries like Estonia, Saudi Arabia and Morocco, we are simultaneously unjustifiably in awe of the ësilky skillsí of the Southern Europeans. In 1997 Leicester and Aston Villa comfortably ëbeatí the spreads in away games against top Spanish opposition though everyone else, notably Liverpool, found it tough living up to their supremacy ratings. This, I believe is a fairly consistent trend and one which warrants some attention.

Major competitions

For the ardent gambler the ultimate football challenges must be the World Cup. The 1998 competition was the biggest sports gambling event ever and the range of spread markets breathtaking. To analyse the ëspecialsí bets alone would have taken most of the duration of the competition. Markets reached new heights of absurdity with the Sporting Index offer of a ëspecial inside priceí to clients singing the title of a market based around match performances of Saudi Arabia, i.e. ëSheikh Rattle and Rollí.

For those inclined to try their hand at backing the winners the spread companies produced some monumental tournament indices. In particular Sporting Index offered a rare *200 Index* whereby 200 points were awarded to the winner, 150 for runner up etc. All 32 teams were quoted. Anyone buying a team on this index, and for that matter any of the companies overall tournament indices, should have considered one factor before trading. On the Sporting *200 Index* there were 950 points to be awarded in total but just prior to the tournament the total of all the sell points was 936 whereas the total of the buy points was 1062. In effect it could be said that all buyers were faced with a horrendous margin in comparison with sellers.

I am sure that a lot of people ëseeí the structure of the World Cup and its smaller brother the European Championships in a false way. On the day of the draw for the 1998 finals the BBC pundit Jimmy Hill stated that looking at the draw it was fairly easy to predict the results of the games prior to them being played (with the exception of Group D which he deemed to close to call). I would certainly be interested had someone taken him up on this challenge as a close inspection of previous World Cup results from the opening group games display patterns which most punters seem to ignore. There is a paradox that though people tend to remember the great giant killing acts of recent World Cups, (Algeria beating West Germany in 1982 or Cameroon beating Argentina in the opening match of 1990), they still tend to give the ëfavouritesí or, more specifically, the top seeds in each group, too much respect in making their forecasts.

In World Cup competitions the seeds in each group have generally performed badly compared to their odds. Looking at competitions since 1970 the top seeds are somewhat more likely not to finish first in their group than they are to win it. In 1994 the group qualification structure was absurd. Twenty four teams played 72 matches to eliminate just eight countries. To find the winners from the remaining 16 countries took just 15 games. Italy, who finished third in their qualification group, managed to reach the final. Thankfully for the 1998 tournament the format reverted to just two qualifiers from each of eight groups. As a qualification place was harder to achieve (since no third placed teams went through) the seeds put on a better performance than in any previous World Cup. It should be noted however that in the first round of games in particular the seeds struggled to match their individual match supremacy predictions implied in the spread quotes.

In looking at the groups initially it is all too easy to fall into the trap of applying a simple formula to the games. One may think along the lines of the top seeds winning all their games, the bottom seeds losing all theirs and the middle two trying to pick up the pieces to scrape into second place. In fact the results of groups tend to be a lot closer than is generally perceived and the performance of the qualifiers consequently poorer than one might expect. A look at what actually happened in the 1994 qualifying groups (a fairly ëtypicalí qualifying competition) highlights this.

Performance of group winners in their three group games

	Won	Drawn	Lost
Romania	2	0	1
Brazil	2	1	0
Germany	2	1	0
Nigeria	2	0	1
Mexico	1	1	1
Netherlands	2	0	1

Performance of group runners up in their group games

	Won	Drawn	Lost
Switzerland	1	1	1
Sweden	1	2	0
Spain	1	2	0
Bulgaria	2	0	1
Ireland	1	1	1
Saudi Arabia	2	0	1

The striking thing about these figures is how little a team has to do to qualify. Of the six winners, four of them managed to lose a game, (none of them won all three), and of the six runners-up four of them only actually beat one other team. The overall message from this is that qualification is something of a lottery. It is liable to be totally unclear who the qualifiers will be coming into the last round of group games and frequently there are rather farcical scenes as the television commentators, not to mention the viewers, are unaware of the various permutations of results that will enable a particular team to qualify.

It is certainly true that the winners of major competitions almost exclusively come from those in the top four of the initial betting. Though with the emphasis on more knockout games in the final stages in recent tournaments, there is an increasing likelihood of an unfancied team going all the way. The truism that the World Cup is always won by a team playing in its home continent should finally be broken for the competition held in South Korea/Japan in 2002 unless there is a major shock.

5 Market Focus: Racing

At first glance these markets are a bewildering prospect. In comparison, fractional odds betting is straightforward.

Racing accounts for around a quarter of all spread bets placed; not a bad share of the market when you consider that the number of big televised events is limited. However, horse racing and Spread Betting are rather uneasy partners. The levies which are currently paid by fractional odds punters as part of the ëtaxí element of their bet contribute directly to the funding of the sport. These levies do not apply to spread stakes, ensuring that racing administrators are not over keen to promote Spread Betting.

A full series of markets are available daily from all the companies on the two top afternoon meetings of the day with a couple of markets on the ëminorí meeting, though occasionally they may differ on their interpretation of which the ëminorí meeting actually is. Thankfully the companies frame the markets in the same way so direct comparisons of quotes can be made. Summer evening cards are extensively covered. Quotes are available around 75 minutes before the first race of a meeting. These are updated following every race so you can take a view on the whole meeting or simply try to make a profit on a single race.

Total SP's (Starting Prices) - The aggregate SPs of the meetings winners, with 1/2 = 0.5; Evens = 1; 2/1 = 2 etc. Prices are rounded up to the nearest first decimal point i.e. 9/4 = 2.3

Double Card Numbers - The aggregate of racecard numbers of the winning horses doubled.

Favourites - Index on favourites being placed in races where 25 points are awarded for a win, 10 for coming second and 5 for coming third.

Total Winning Lengths - Aggregate winning distances (distances in lengths between the horse finishing first and second). For distances below 1/2 length the following decimals apply: Head/Nose = 0.1; Head = 0.2; Neck = 0.3.

Jockey/Trainer Performance - 25 points for every race won; 10 for second; 5 for 3rd.

At first glance these markets are a bewildering prospect. In comparison, fractional odds betting is straightforward - pick your fancy for any given race and get paid out according to the odds if it wins. In Spread Betting the relative merits of the runners assume lesser importance; you rarely find yourself willing one particular runner to win and, as such, betting on the racing spreads is a vastly different affair to fractional odds betting.

To be successful it is important to have a clear rationale as to why one is having a spread bet. The ëbig ideaí behind any bet has to include some element that, in your assessment, has not been taken into account in the framing of a quote. It is not enough to flick through the estimates of SPís in the morning paper and blindly decide to buy the favourites market because there are a couple of strong odds on chances running - all this is built into the quotes.

Say you believe that a favourite that is listed in the morning paper with an SP forecast of 3/1 is going to dramatically shorten in the odds when the on course betting market opens. Assuming you believe it will win you may have a legitimate tactic to buy the Favouriteís market a few minutes before betting shows are available as you will be one step ahead of the spread companies who have only ëallowedí for a weak favourite.

The spread markets are very dependent upon the estimated strengths of the runners as presented by the SP forecasts in the press. If you want to estimate the SPís of the winners in a particular meeting prior to the start then you are probably going to rely on the SP forecast published in the morning paper. (*Racing Post* SP forecasts are displayed on BBC Ceefax). For all the markets, except those on winning distances, there are means by which you can analyse the SP forecasts for meetings and arrive at a mathematically ëcorrectí assessment of the market. With pen and paper these calculations are somewhat laboured and you are likely to run up against the paradox that the more powerful your prediction methods the closer you are to replicating the precise model that the spread companies are using. Hence you spend two hours in a morning arriving at the exactly the same figures as the quotes of the companies.

If you really fancy your hand at stats you may be tempted to try to come up with a model for calculating markets that has more predictive potential than that of the spread companies, though I dare say this could become a lifeís work.

Under the spread firmsí rules the published SP forecasts in the racing press actually determine SPís where races do not take place. Forecasts differ from paper to paper, though in general they are a reasonably fair reflection of the odds that the runners open at. There is however a pronounced tendency for clear favourites to shorten drastically. A paper forecast of 6/4 for the favourite where the second favourite is rated at 11/4 (i.e. there isnít much doubt over which the favourite will be), can easily lead to the favourite opening on the course at evens or less.

My guess is that a lot of clear favourites get backed heavily in the betting shops in the morning, particularly as part of multiple bets. The representatives of the large bookmaking firms make sure that these runners open at even shorter prices by placing money on-course. This difficulty is particularly relevant to the SPs and Favourites markets where a correct estimate of the SP of the favourite is vital. It is also worth bearing in mind that for most of the markets non-runners can make an enormous difference, particularly if they are favourites, so one should check non-runners updates without fail prior to placing any bet.

Winning SP'S

The SPís market is a close cousin of the market on favourites. If we assume that favourites, on average, have SPs in the region of 2/1 then the smallest make-up on the SPís market on a six race card must be around 12 (six races x SP make-up of two per race). If the extraordinary happens and six totally unfancied outsiders romp home at 33/1 then the make-up is potentially pushing 200.

If offered a quote on the SPís market of 27-30 at the beginning of a six race card, how is it possible to accurately assess how this quote is reached? The opening quotes of a meeting are simply a total of the quotes for the individual races, but at the start of the meeting there is no way of ëseparatingí out which elements of the quotes relate to which race. Simply dividing the midpoint of the quote (28.5) by the number of races (six) gives us a rough average of 4.75 per race, but it is possible to look much closer at the estimated make-up for each race.

Taking a three runner race as our initial example:

	Estimated odds	**make-up if winner**
Natural Park	Evens (50%)	1
Mr Music Man	3/1 (25%)	3
Frantic Tan	3/1 (25%)	3

The SP of the winner can only make-up at one or three but the ëcorrectí estimate of the make-up is a weighted average of all the possible make-ups.

This type of calculation keeps cropping up in the racing spreads and is worth spending a bit of time getting to grips with. To find the weighted average we first multiply the percentage for the odds of each horse by the make-up if it should win:

Natural Park	50% x 1 =	50
Mr Music Man	25% x 3 =	75
Frantic Tan	25% x 3 =	75
	100%	200

The sum of [percentage x make-ups] is divided by [sum of percentage] to give us an estimated make-up for the race of two (200/100 = 2). The fact that it is impossible for a make-up of two to actually happen (assuming the SPs turn out like the forecasts) may be perplexing, but nevertheless, if this was the first of the six race card mentioned before then two points are being ëallowed forí in the spread. If the initial quote was 27-30 then this race accounts for two points of that quote.

Imagine a situation where the odds on the first race were markedly different and one of the horses was a very strong odds on favourite:

	Estimated odds	make-up if winner
Natural Park	1/4 (80%)	0.25
Mr Music Man	9/1 (10%)	9
Frantic Tan	9/1 (10%)	9

In this example it might look at first glance that the estimated SP of the winner should be lower as the favourite is so strong. Going through the weighted average calculation, however, demonstrates that the estimated SP is, in fact, the same.

(N.B. so that the figures are exact I have used the ëpreciseí make-up figure of 0.25 for the 1/4 horse though in practice this is rounded up to 0.3)

Natural Park	80% x 0.25	=	20
Mr Music Man	10% x 9	=	90
Frantic Tan	10% x 9	=	90
	100%		200

It theoretically doesnít matter what the relative merits of the horses are, the estimated make-up for the three runner race always remains at two. This leads to a more general rule concerning the relationship between the number of runners in a race and the estimated SP of the winner. You may have noticed that the SP total percentages in the above examples add up to only 100%. In real life this is rarely going to happen as the bookmaker builds in a margin to his odds. This ensures that the actual odds offered are lower than the genuine chance of an individual runner winning. However it is useful to remember that if the book is ëfairí (the total percentages of the odds add up to 100%) then the SP of the winner should equal the number of runners in a race, minus one. So in a 11 runner race the best estimate of the SP make-up would be 10.

In a race where the total percentages of all the runners equals 150% (just about the maximum one should come across) then the odds on offer will be substantially lower than the ërealí odds. Here the SP of the winner would perhaps be expected to make-up at half the number of runners. The number of runners is closely related to the total SP percentage; the more runners in a race the higher this percentage.

Handicap races will almost always have a higher SP percentage than non handicap races with the same number of runners. There is an additional factor which is harder to quantify which has to be taken account of. The calculation of the estimated SP using the weighted average of the odds assumes that the same degree of margin is built into all the odds equally. Level stakes on runners in certain price brackets perform worse than others. The worst performing group are horses who are in the bottom half of the betting, though people tend to instinctively look to the longer odds selections in search of value. A £1 stake on all the outsiders through a large number of races will see your bank plummet.

The implication of this on the spreads is quite significant. The fact that horses at longer prices perform badly in relation to their odds alters the way in which we must assess the likely make-up of the SP. In addition, the fact the the bookmakers margin increases with the number of entrants in a race effectivley means that the prices in large fields are significantly lower than the ëtrueí chances of any given runner. Taking these factors into account you will find that, in general, the following formulae apply:

❑   In races up to eight runners the average SP of the winner = number of runners multiplied by 0.6

❑   In races with 9 -12 runners the average SP of the winner = number of runners multiplied by 0.55

❑   In races up to 13 - 16 runners the average SP of the winner = number of runners multiplied by 0.5

❑   In races of over 17 runners the average SP of the winner = number of runners multiplied by 0.45

Therefore in a 11 runner race you might expect the estimated SP of the winner to equal 11 x 0.55 = 6.05. The vital element of assessing the SPs of the winners therefore has little to do with the relative merits of the horses but is mostly dependent on the number of horses in a race. There is only one opportunity in a meeting of getting a good feel for how the market operates precisely; just prior to the last race on the card. Here the quotes are ëuncontaminatedí by other races.

		profit or (loss) for sellers	profit or (loss) for buyers
Mr Softy	2/1	1	(2)
Once Down	3/1	0	(1)
Maverick	3/1	0	(1)
Celestial Choir	6/1	(3)	2
Island Dreams	8/1	(5)	4

The quote is at 32 - 33 following the previous races and the total now stands at 29. Taking the prices at face value the weighted mean calculation suggests the make-up allowance for this race should be 3.6. Using our adjusted formula (number of runners x 0.6) we reach the slightly lower value of 3.0. This effectively takes into account the fact that the two outsiders have somewhat less chance than their odds imply. The significance of the one point margin in the spread is considerable.

This example is based on a genuine race and illustrates how the fortunes of buyers and sellers can fluctuate. Here the sell position is terrible; a measly one point profit should the favourite win and a downside of three and five points on the two outsiders. The buy position has a total potential win of six points with a downside of just four. These type of situations happen every day but as quotes contain elements from all the other races, apart from the last race of the card, they do not make themselves known easily. Selling SPs can be a fraught business because the vast majority of runners are against you.

Winning Lengths

A bet on winning distances requires you to watch a race in an entirely new way. The usual excitement factor of willing on a particular horse is altogether banished in favour of a different desire to see the horses cross the line with as much gap between first and second as possible (as a buyer) or all in a line with the judge left with an impossible task of finding the winner (as a seller). In terms of excitement it is difficult to beat though it requires some sober assessment beforehand.

Watching the closing stages of a run-of-the-mill, 10-runner, seven-furlong, flat race, you are, more often than not, going to find four or five horses in contention with a furlong left and perhaps three making a serious effort in the last 50 yards. In our fictitious example the leading horse goes clear by a length then eases off slightly in the last few paces allowing the second and third places horses to come back within 1/2 a length. Having watched a few races which follow fairly similar patterns (including some close fought handicaps) you are asked to estimate the average winning distances in flat races. Where would you pitch it? My instinctive reaction would have been to say just under a length, remembering that most photo finishes will be assigned a make-up of 0.1. I was surprised that following a race in which the wining distance was just over a length, (which intuitively appeared to be quite a large margin of victory), the spread actually went down by 0.5.

In fact the mean winning distance on the flat is, from stats I have available, 1.75 lengths. This instinctively appears somewhat too high, but to clarify what is happening here I have presented a random sample of race make-ups taken from flat meetings in 1997.

(Figures in brackets are the number of runners)

0.2 (6)	0.1 (18)	1.3 (10)	0.3 (7)	0.5 (22)	1.0 (17)
0.5 (20)	1.3 (14)	**5.0** (11)	1.3 (9)	1.5 (8)	0.3 (20)
1.5 (21)	0.2 (8)	1.5 (5)	0.5 (9)	0.3 (10)	0.75 (21)
0.5 (16)	**2.5** (5)	1.2 (12)	0.5 (20)	0.75 (14)	**4.0** (20)
0.3 (19)	0.3 (19)	0.5 (3)	0.3 (6)	0.3 (7)	1.25 (5)
4.0 (3)	**6.0** (10)	1.3 (9)	**8.0** (10)	1.0 (10)	1.5 (9)
0.3 (7)	1.3 (7)	0.2 (11)	**4.0** (8)	1.5 (10)	**2.5** (5)
0.5 (10)	**4.0** (5)	**4.5** (10)	1.5 (7)	**6.0** (7)	**4.5** (6)
1.0 (6)	0.5 (5)	0.5 (5)	0.3 (13)	**8.0** (8)	0.3 (9)
1.5 (11)	1.5 (9)	0.75 (8)	**2.5** (8)	**4.5** (13)	**4.0** (10)
1.3 (6)	0.75 (9)	**2.5** (5)	0.3 (6)	0.2 (18)	1.3(10)
0.75 (7)	1.5 (22)	1.5 (13)	1.0 (19)	**3.5** (8)	1.3 (18)

The mean of all the 72 distances is 1.72 lengths, close enough to my general calculation of 1.75 lengths to assume it is a reasonably representative sample. However, I have highlighted the very few figures that are actually above this mean - just 18 in total (25%). It as therefore no wonder that it is possible to get an impression that the mean is lower than it really is, as you can watch the vast majority of races end well below the mean. The distribution of results is severely skewed with only a handful of ëfreakishí results (two of eight lengths in particular) tugging the mean upwards.

If we were to imagine that each row is a separate six race meeting where the midpoint of the quote conforms to the general mean, we might expect to receive a quote of 10-11. If we were to sell on each of the 12 occasions we would be winning on eight of them and losing only on the remaining four. If youíre not keen on enduring long losing runs then buying winning distances is to be avoided. As a seller the trick is to try and avoid the handful of unpleasantly high distances.

There are two factors that have a significant bearing on both flat and jumpsí winning distances. The whole thrust of the handicapping system is to try and even-out differences of ability between runners. Ultimately the handicapper has done has job admirably if 22 runners finish simultaneously. Indeed winning distances in handicap races are approximately 25% less than those in non-handicaps. The number of runners in a race obviously also has a bearing. If you are a seller then avoid races with less than four declared runners at all costs - not so much because the small field isnít taken account of in the initial quotes, but rather the slight risk of runners being withdrawn and a walkover resulting. Under spread companies rules this is declared as a five length win for flat races and 12 for National Hunt racing.

In general, as the going gets softer, the winning distances grow larger. The following figures are taken from a sample of over 2500 races at 10 British courses:

Mean Winning Distances on varying ground conditions (Declared going/Mean winning lengths):

Firm	Good to Firm	Good	Good/Soft	Soft	Heavy
1.58	1.68	1.83	1.97	2.46	2.78

Though the sample of meetings declared ësoftí and ëheavyí is far smaller than for those declared on the ëgoodí side there is an almost perfect linear relationship between going and winning distances.

When watching the finish of a race you may be surprised at how the official declaration of distances consistently appears smaller than a visual estimate. This is due to the fact that the distance is calculated by extrapolating from the difference in timings, not by visual means.

In my experience races on firm ground are particularly susceptible to this apparent ëunderestimationí of distances.

There is also a tendency for the *Winning Lengths* market to be brought up when there is a lot of wet weather around, though I am not convinced this is justified. My reading of the way in which quotes are framed is that the means are calculated with some of the ësoft ground elementí within them at all times and in all weathers. In other words, when the sun shines, think seriously about a sell, when it doesnít, steer clear. This observation is reinforced by my general impression that the make-ups tend to end up on the sell-side of the initial quotes when the quote started low in the first place. (For a six race card I would deem a ëlowí quote to be under 10). When flat quotes start off high (over 13 lengths for a six card meeting) the proportion of make-ups that finish on either side of the initial quotes seem to be more equally balanced.

Opening quote	Make-up	Opening Quote	Make-up
9-10	6.45	13.5-15	14.1
11.5-12.5	9.2	14.5-15.5	19.9
9.5-10.5	2.65	10-11	12
10-11	13.75	14.5-16	24.65
11-12	7.55	20-22	10
11.5-12.5	13	19-21	11.5
8.5-9.5	5.15	14-15.5	16.6
13-14	9.5	15.5-16	12.85
11-12	3.8	14-15.5	8.95
12.5-13.5	12.5	16-17.5	20.75
12-13	6	21-23	11.65
10.5-11.5	6.05	10-11	5.55
10-11	10.05	17.5-19	18.9
12-13	8.35	14-15	8.8
13.5-14.5	6.45	15.5-16.5	10.75

The above is a log of quotes on flat meeting winning distances over a period of a month from mid-September to mid-October, just prior to the end of the flat season. The summer had been unspectacular in terms of heat and dryness but consistently selling winning distances would have resulted in a fairly large profit. By the middle of September things were quiet on the weather front and the vast majority of meetings were declared good or good to firm. The second column commences on Oct. seventh with six meetings where the heavens opened and for a week the ground was very much on the soft side. The prices quoted were available generally and constitute a rough average of all the companiesí prices.

The first column is a sellers dream - only two small losses and a profit of over 50 points. Jump over to the rainy week in the second column and some significant high make-upís creep in. Not too much reliance should be placed on the official declaration of ground conditions. During the wet spell I noticed that ground declarations hardly budged from the conditions declared in the warmer weather. ëGood to firmí became ëgood to firm in placesí when subjectively the difference in weather/ ground conditions seemed to be vast.

My enthusiasm for the Winning Distances market turns lukewarm when it comes to the National Hunt season. Over the jumps the distances rocket and the range is huge. A non-handicap chase would be expected to produce the largest variation of the lot. There is generally a limit of 30 lengths placed by the spread companies on any one race make-up over the jumps (12 on the flat). The maximum distance is rarely approached on the flat but on a boggy winterís day it is fairly common to see a horse storm clear by 20 or more lengths. This makes the jumps distances very heavily geared and open to chance. In a seven race meeting the final make-up has a realistic range of anywhere between five and 140 lengths - a daunting proposition. It might be supposed that when a favourite is very strongly odds-on in a jumps race it is liable to storm home by a mile. My suspicion is that enough people jump on this factor to swing the market too far in the buy direction. Consequently most of the value to be found in such races is on the sell side.

There is increasing concern in jockey club circles that Spread Betting, particularly that on winning distance, may ëcompromiseí the jockeys. It is not unusual to see a horse in a strong lead drop down a couple of gears as it approaches the winning line, particularly as this might find favour with the handicapper, but **it is quite conceivable that a jockey could be tempted to 'manipulate' the winning distance**.

Double Card Numbers

Each horse in a race is assigned a saddle cloth number. These are used to form the basis for a spread on each meeting. The market on *Double Card Numbers* requires you to predict the total numbers of the winners, doubled. The fact that they are doubled simply makes it more volatile and heavily geared. So if number three was to win every race of a six race meeting the make-up for each race would be six, the total for all races 36 (6x6). It is worth bearing in mind that some races have a disproportionate effect on the overall make-up. The significance of a four runner race where the make-up can be between two and eight is dwarfed by a race with 21 runners where the possible make-upís are between two and 42.

In a four runner race there must be four potential make-upís:
> 2 if number 1 wins
> 4 if number 2 wins
> 6 if number 3 wins
> 8 if number 4 wins

We can say that the average make-up for this race should be the total number of possible make-up figures divided by the number of runners (20 divided by 4 = 5 average make-up). So if a spread was to be set we might expect a quote of 4.5 - 5.5. Clearly if we think number two or number four will win we would want to sell at 4.5. Conversely buying at 5.5 would put us in profit if number three or four won. This is fine if all four horses were rated as having an equal chance but what if one horse is an overwhelming favourite? To arrive at a correct estimate we have to use an average which is weighted by the relative chances of the runners. For example suppose our four runners were rated as follows in the betting:

Number 1	Lucky Fellow	4/5
Number 2	Mustabar	3/1
Number 3	Insapio	16/1
Number 4	Lunar Horizon	4/1

If we had a chance to sell at 4.5 here we would jump at the opportunity. The hot favourite and second favourite are both on the sell side. To arrive at a ëcorrectí assessment of where the spread should be we need to take the prices into account. Back to our weighted average calculation:

		odds	**%**	**% x m/u per horse**
Number 1	Lucky Fellow	4/5	(55.6%)	(55.6 x 2) = 111.2
Number 2	Mustabar	3/1	(25%)	(25 x 4) = 100
Number 3	Insapio	16/1	(5.9%)	(5.9 x 6) = 35.4
Number 4	Lunar Horizon	4/1	(20%)	(20 x 8) = 160
		total =	**106.5**	**total = 406.6**

406.6 divided by all total percentages (106.5) = 3.8 mean make-up

The odds are first translated into their percentage figures. This gives the numerical indication of the strength of the horse. We then multiply each percentage by the make-up should the horse win. The total of these is divided by the total of the percentages. What we end up with is a theoretical make-up for the race of 3.8. We might therefore expect a spread of 3.3 - 4.3 on this race. Obviously it must be lower than the previous average of five that we gained from the example when all four runners were deemed to be of the same ability. This time a sell at 3.3 would only profit if Lucky Fellow came first, giving you a modest win of 1.3 points. Any other result would lose. A win for Lunar Horizon would have a downside for the seller of 4.7.

There are good reasons why it is important to accurately assess the mean make-up for a race. As previously pointed out it is not all that easy to actually back a particular horse to win on the spreads. *Double Card Numbers* does offer an opportunity to back a particular selection but, as with all gambling, it is important to know what ëpriceí you are getting. In the cut and thrust of the spread market this is not instantly obvious. If you fancy number 11 High Mood to win the 3.30 at a minor meeting on a Wednesday afternoon then backing your judgement on the spreads is a little more involved than scribbling the name of the horse on a betting slip at your local bookie.

Take a situation where the spread is at 78 - 80 after four races of a six race card. So far the make-ups have totalled 60. In the next race the betting is as follows:

1	Boots Madden	11/4
2	Lady High Sheriff	10/1
3	Who am I	14/1
4	Majors Legacy	12/1
5	Indian Delight	14/1
6	Millersford	8/1
7	Blue Laws	14/1
8	Finnigan Free	16/1
9	Capenwray	5/1
10	Winnow	10/1
11	High Mood	12/1
12	Country Store	16/1

We are considering buying the Double Numbers index at 80 as we think the make-up of the next race will be on the high side (hopefully 22 if number 11 High Mood wins). The plan is then to sell back at a profit. But how do we know the potential profit in such a trade?

The first step to be able to tell what the spread companies are ëallowingí in their quote for the next race. The difference between the current quote of 78 - 80 (midpoint 79) and the total make-ups so far (60) is what the firm ëexpectí to be the make-upís of the last two races combined, in this case 29. To discover what they are allowing for the next race, and therefore how the spread might change following the result, we need to perform the calculation for our previous four horse example. The number crunching yields an average make-up figure of nine.

If all the horses were deemed to be of equal ability the mean make-up value would be 13; we can therefore see that the favourite Boots Madden who is assigned number one (a potential make-up of two) has significantly lowered the expected make-up. We can think of this figure of nine as the ëallowanceí the spread firm has made for the race. Therefore, adding nine on the total make-ups so far (60) gives 69 as the expected total make-ups following this next race. Since the spread stands at 78 - 80 (midpoint 79) we can also deduce that the expected make-up of the final race on the card will be: 79 minus 69 = expected make-up of final race of, 10.

Now we have a fair idea of the expected make-up of the race we are interested in, we can assess the various outcomes of backing our selection, number 11, High Mood. If High Mood wins, 22 will be added to the make-up total, bringing it to 82. This is 13 above the expected make-up of nine so we can expect to be about 13 points up on the spread. High Mood romps home and the spread is updated. The total stands at 82 with an allowance of 10 for the final race so the spread should be in the region of 91.5 - 92.5. If we had previously bought the index at 80 we could now sell back at 91.5 for a 11.5 point profit.

We could also calculate the effect of other results. If the expected make-up is nine then any winning horse higher than number four should put us in a profit position. If the favourite won (number one) with a make-up of two we would be: 9 - 2 = 7 points down. This would be reflected in the new spread when updated. There are times when Double Numbers trading comes into its own if you have a particular fancy in a race.

In the above example we particularly benefited because the make-up (if our chosen horse won) was 13 points out of line with the expected make-up. However there are clearly situations in which other avenues are better explored, depending on the circumstances. Going back to our last example; letís say we fancied number four Majors Legacy at 12/1. Here we are hoping for a make-up of 8 but that it just about plumb where the mean make-up stands anyway so there is really no trade to be had.

It is difficult to see the attraction of betting through the card with *Double Card Numbers*. It is unlikely that a situation would arise in where you would conclude that making a trade on *Double Card Numbers* would manage to beat the spread over the course of the meeting, though it should be noted that race card numbers are not randomly assigned to the runners. The heaviest weight is assigned the lowest number.

There is a generally accepted theory that low weight horses (those with high numbers) are more successful on soft/heavy ground. The *Double Card Numbers* market may therefore give an opportunity to trade on this type of premise.

Favourites Index

M any horse racing systems and truisms are based on the
performance of the favourite horse. Indeed, in analysing any
single race the key element is probably whether the favourite is going
to perform up to expectation. All the spread companies operate a
Favourites Index whereby 25 points is added for a winning favourite,
10 if it finishes second, 5 if it finishes third and 0 for a finish outside
the top three.

The way points are assigned is significantly different from the place
structure in traditional odds betting. Odds in place betting are generally either a fifth (20%) or a fourth (25%) the odds of the win. A second position on the spread earns 40% of the value of the win (10 points
for second being 40% of the 25 points awarded). A third position is
worth 20% of the rewards for a win. Generally speaking the spreads
are much more generous for a horse placed second than the place odds
you receive in traditional betting, though considerably worse for horses
placed third. No points are assigned for fourth place on the spreads
though in larger fields you would receive 1/4 the odds at the bookies.

There is a lot of speculation as to which courses are generally the best/
worst for favourites. The one way **not** to set about this is simply to take
the percentage of winning favourites against the number of races. It all
depends what price the favourite starts at. It is clearly unreasonable to
compare a 13/2 favourite in a 20 runner handicap with a 2/7 shot in a 2
1/2 mile chase. The only fair way to look at it is to express the favour-
itesí success in terms of what your return would be for a fixed stake on
every favourite on the course in question.

In general, favourites win around 37% of all races. By betting exclusively on favourites you may lose between 1% and 55% of your stake
depending on which course it is. It is the case that favourites in handicap races, are slightly worse value than non-handicap races though this
may be due to the fact that handicaps generally have a higher number
of runners making the total SP percentage more difficult to overcome.
The Racing Post gives an excellent summary of the fate of favourites
over the past year for all the meetings of the day. These are well worth
referring to when considering a bet on this market.

Lower grade racing often produces favourites which perform poorly compared to their prices, though this is certainly not a hard and fast rule. The All-weather tracks at Southwell, Lingfield and Wolverhampton come in the bottom five for favourites performance against SP. Newbury and Sandown, which tend to host reasonably good quality racing, come out on top over a long period, but only just ahead of centres of lesser excellence at Folkestone and Brighton.

The spread must reflect that favourites will start at varying prices. Imagine that the first race on the card is a five runner affair:

Total Asset	evs
Grand Applause	2/1
Tiger Lake	4/1
Not to Panic	20/1
Zander	20/1

The spread starts the afternoon at 74-78. The favourite, Total Asset, wins and as a result the spread moves up to 84-94. This effectively means that the favourite did 10 points better than expected, suggesting the expected make-up for the race was 15. In the event of it finishing outside the top three the spread to fall by 15 points (i.e. it performed 15 points worse than expected). In either case it becomes clear that 15 points were allowed in the spread for its performance.

In general the following allowances apply:

Favourites price	Points allowance
1/2	18
4/7	17
4/5	16
evs	15
5/4	14
6/4	13
7/4	12
2/1	11
5/2	10
3/1	9
4/1	8
5/1	7

If you have a six race card where the favourites are rated at evens, 3/1, 6/4, 2/1, 3/1 and 7/4 it should be quite easy to deduce that the allowances are approximately $15 + 9 + 13 + 11 + 9 + 12$ giving a total quote with a mid-point of 69.

The only proviso with this table is that favourites in very small fields need to be allocated slightly more points. Imagine a two runner race where the favourite is 1/2 and the other runner is 6/4. Clearly the favourite cannot make-up at anything but 25 for first place or 10 for second as there are only two runners. The spread allowance from the table would assign 18 to the favourite though this would suggest that his chance of finishing first was only just better than his chances of finishing second. In this case an allowance of around 20.5 would be more appropriate.

There is a quick calculation that you can perform to see if a particular quote is in line with the SP forecasts. This relates the quote to the strength of the days favourites. Going back to our mythical six race card:

	Estimated Price of Favourite	**%**
first race	Evens	50%
second race	3/1	25%
third race	6/4	40%
fourth race	2/1	33%
fifth race	3/1	25%
sixth race	7/4	36%
Total % (strength of favourites) =		209

If the favourites are at longish odds then the strength figure will be a lot lower, and correspondingly higher if the favourites are at shorter odds. The trick is to divide this strength figure by the mid-point of the quote.

$$\frac{209}{69} = 3.03$$

The range for this final factor is 2.5-3.4. We can see this factor as a measure of how close the quote corresponds to the strength of the favourites.

If the factor is towards the lower end of its range then the index is on the high side in relation to the SP forecasts. In this case there may be an argument for selling the index. If the factor is towards the top end of the range then favourites are undervalued and it might be worth considering a buy on the index.

Examination of these factors will lead you to the conclusion that strong favourites tend to be slightly undervalued in the spread market and weak favourites overvalued. This could be due to any number of factors. Very strong favourites tend to run in small fields where there is a low total percentage overound on the book, therefore horses perform very well compared to their SPís. In a 22 runner handicap the overound is probably massive (approaching 150%) so the 4/1 favourite, like all the other horses in the race, has considerably less chance than the SP suggests.

Another point relevant to the general performance of favourites is the weather. The table below illustrates how favourites performance deteriorates as the going gets worse:

Mean make-up figures for favourites on varying ground conditions

Ground conditions	Firm	Good/Firm	Good	Good/Soft	Soft
Mean make-up	14.1	11.0	8.0	6.5	7.2

The variation is highly significant. Even discounting the firm ground and soft ground figures (which are based on a much smaller sample) the difference between the value of 11 for ground declared to be good/firm and the value of 6.5 for good/soft is huge in Spread Betting terms. If you multiply the difference (4.5) over a six race meeting it totals a variation of 27 points alone, about 40% of the usual total spread value itself.

There are two conflicting arguments concerning the position of very strong odds on favourites. Alan Potts, author of *Against the Crowd* has an interesting theory about ësure thingsí. Any horse, he states, has a chance of suffering from some unforeseen problem, whether it be interference, burst blood vessel, lameness etc. These difficulties are just as likely to affect a hot favourite as a long shot. If up to 25% of runners are affected in this way then the short odds backer is running an enormous risk. A horse at 1/2 only returns 1.5 times your stake yet you are effectively risking 50% of your potential winnings on it being fit and well enough to run to its form. To the longer odds backer this risk accounts for a comparatively tiny proportion of potential winnings and therefore is less significant.

This seems like a very reasoned judgement, though a look at the performance figures for strong odds on favourites reveals that, re-markably, they perform exceptionally well compared to their SPs. Taking a sample of close on 10,000 races from 1996/1997, figures suggest that the best ëvalueí horses are in fact those whose starting prices are around 1/2. Backing these horses, without paying tax, produces a net loss of only 2 - 3% whereas losses on horses with SPs at the 2/1 mark would have been 6 - 7%. The worst performing horses were outsiders - indiscriminately backing 16/1 shots would have seen you lose over 50% of your stake. This goes against com-mon belief, which suggests that it is horses ranking second and third in the betting market which offer the most value.

There has been some discussion of the subject of ëfalseí steamers and false ëfavouritesí. Undoubtedly many steamers (horses whose odds sharply drop) are caused by a few moderate bets placed early morning by those individuals who the large bookmaking firms are wary of. This causes an immediate contraction of the odds causing TV pundits to make a comment. This in turn causes the betting shop fraternity to get on (so as not to miss a ëgood thingí) causing further price falls. As a result, the horse that the shrewdies took at 20/1 in the morning (as they thought it was more like a 10/1 chance), ends up with an unjustifiably short SP in the region of 5/1. False favourites are easier for the spread bettor to oppose. If you have done your homework and identified a favourite, particularly one that the public seem keen to back in droves (whether it be because of its colour, popular trainer etc.), the *Favour-ites Index* allows you to back your judgement precisely.

There is slight evidence to suggest that selling the *Favourites Index* is a sound long term policy. The *Favourites Index* makes-up lower than the initial quote on roughly 10% more occasions than it makes-up higher, resulting in a small profit. This characteristic was particularly notice-able in the most recent flat racing season. Strangely, in monitoring the spreads, there was at the same time a marked tendency for SPs to make-up at lower than the original quotes. This seems something of a contradiction as you might expect bad performances by favourites to cause the average SPs to rise.

Looking at the figures a little closer one can see the optimum quotes for selling favourites were when the quote was low to begin with (the same characteristic as the Winning Distances market), i.e. where the races on the card contained a disproportionate number of favourites at high forecast SPs. These, inevitably tend to be races with large fields. I would term a quote of under 60 as ëlowí for a six race card. This suggests that the favourites are forecast to have SPís, on average, of around 5/2. Where the initial quote was 80 or higher favourites performed well enough to justify their low forecast SPís. My general perception, therefore, is to go low when the favourites market is low to start with. This takes a bit of nerve as an initial look at a low market reveals that only two winning favourites, with one other favourite placed, is enough to make-up the market at above the sell point.

One of the possible pitfalls of the Favourites Market is the treatment of joint favourites. The declaration of joint favourites is a fairly common occurrence; rather than splitting the points the spread companies simply declare that the favourite is the horse with the lowest card number. This could give rise to serious problems if you want to back against a particular ëfavouriteí. If two horses are heading the betting just prior to the off:

Number 4	Challenger du Luc	5/4
Number 3	Amtrack Express	13/8

You believe that the ëfavouriteí, Challenger du Luc, is going to come nowhere so you sell the index. The trouble is that other people are thinking along the same lines and putting money on Amtrack Express, which goes into 6/4. To compensate, Challenger du Luc drifts out to 6/4 and suddenly they are the same price. Your hunch is correct - Amtrack Express wins by a mile. To your horror you realise that it is Amtrack Express who is deemed favourite by the spread companies as it has a lower card number. So 25 points is added to the *Favourites Index* and you are staring at a loss even though you read the race correctly.

Strategies For Backing Individual Horses

It is clear that backing a horse to win on the spreads can be a complicated business. If you intend to use Spread Betting to state a preference for a particular horse there are a number of avenues to look at, depending on which markets are offered and the shape of a particular race. It is comparatively easy to back a horse in a major televised race. The feature races in televised meetings are subject to index quotes, usually 50:25:10 indices awarded for the first, second and third horses home respectively. In a race of 10 runners or less you may find all the runners listed. Where there are more than 10 runners, there may be a quote on ëThe Fieldí which includes all the other runners (the outsiders). On this sort of index it is easy to buy your particular fancy. Also on televised races the spread companies will offer a number of ëmatchí bets. A pair of horses in the same race are paired together with a quote on the finishing distance between them, irrespective of their actual finishing positions:

One Man/Suny Bay 0.5 - 1.5

If you think Suny Bay will beat One Man then you must sell One Manís supremacy at 0.5. If Suny Bay finishes second but a clear four lengths in front of One Man in sixth then your profit is 0.5 plus 4 lengths = 4.5 points.

These situations are relatively straightforward but will only present themselves on televised meetings. To back a horse to win on a wet Monday at Wincanton requires a bit more forethought. Generally the most heavily geared market is on the performance of favourites so it is wise to look here first. If you think you have found a particularly undervalued favourite then you should clearly buy the *Favourites Index*. This is, of course, with the proviso that you must be very sure that your horse is actually going to start as the favourite. Assuming that your favourite is in the region of 2/1 you are going to profit by at least 12 points by buying the *Favourites Index* immediately before the race in question, and selling back before the next race on the card. You are highly unlikely to manage a 12 point profit by trading in any of the other markets.

If you have no particular selection in mind, but are sure that the favourite is overvalued and likely to be beaten, you might consider selling the *Favourites Index*. However, there are difficulties with this strategy. Our favourite at 2/1 might be given an allowance of 11 points on the market. If it ëlosesí the next most likely position it will come is second giving it a make-up of 10. A seller here really needs the favourite to finish third or nowhere at all to make a decent profit. There are unlikely to be rich rewards for getting the favourite beaten into second place unless its estimated SP is very heavily odds on.

In numerical terms the majority of all fractional odds bets are probably on second and third favourites. If you are looking to back a horse in this sort of price range, then the options available will vary from race to race. A look at the SPs market is likely to prove fairly fruitless as the SPs allowed for in the spread will tend to average near the value at which the second and third favourites are placed in the market. The best chance of finding a bet is probably on the *Double Card Numbers* market. Here there are two tests which need to be applied. Is the card number of your chosen horse significantly different from that of the favourite? And, is the card number of your chosen horse significantly different from the weighted mean of the card numbers?

1	Pericles	6/4
2	Plan For Profit	6/1
3	Brutal Fantasy	10/1
4	Fayik	16/1
5	Suatach	16/1
6	Jibereen	16/1
7	Trojan Hero	5/1
8	Suez Tornado	11/4

This structure of race would provide the perfect opportunity for backing second favourite Suez Tornado on the *Double Card Numbers* market. Just over eight points will be allowance in the market (the weighted mean). The favourite is number one, whilst your tip is as far away as possible in the numbers at eight. You buy *Double Card Num-*

bers expecting Suez Tornado to win. Should you be correct you are looking at a make-up of 16 and a profit of about seven points on the market and, in addition, you have other runners who can put you in the money. This sort of bet really comes into its own when there a plenty of runners making the gearing larger.

The spreads are not the place to back individual runners at big prices. If you wish to back a horse that is not fancied in the market you might consider buying the SPs quote. If your horse is rated at 16/1 in a race where the favourite is 2/1 you might be looking at a profit of around 12 points. All in all you would probably be better backing a horse at that sort of price down at your local betting shop as the rewards will be proportionally a lot greater. Spread Betting particularly falls down when it comes to backing a horse to be placed. Apart from the big race indices there is no equivalent to place betting on the spreads, everything revolves around the actual winner.

There are constant accusations levelled against the high street bookmakers that they do everything in their power to promote indiscriminate betting. **This discourages any serious attempts on the part of punters to correctly assess form.** The sheer number of races on an average afternoon provides the fatally addictive attraction to most punters; by the time they seen their fancy fall at Windsor there is barely a couple of minutes to get a bet on the 3.30 at Lingfield and maybe only a brief pause before the bell goes for the 3.33 at Monmore.

Perhaps only 5% of all who wager on horses actually come to their own conclusions. Most rely on racing correspondents in the press, tipping agencies and a variety of what one might loosely regard as ësystemsí. A system is defined as a set of rules that one applies to wagers regardless of the relative merits of the horses themselves. They vary from ridiculous money making schemes that are advertised in the ëbusiness opportunityí columns of newspapers, to ones which are genuinely based on sound rationale and if pursued correctly will usually yield profits. Systems based on the varying of stakes are no more than a crude illusion. If you usually lose 20% of your stakes on selections there is no way that varying your stakes on individual horses will improve your general performance. Varying of stakes shams have yet, to my knowledge, been touted in relation to Spread Betting but as the number of account holders increases you can be sure that there will be those who wish to peddle a variety of useless schemes.

Like systems themselves, tipsters who ask for money to have access to their wisdom are split into those that are complete cons and those who are genuinely on to something - though the former heavily outweigh the latter. In the complete ëconsí bracket are some heavily promoted premium rate tipping lines whose claimed winners may be correct, but whose many losers are conveniently forgotten about, therefore concealing large losses. Many of the subscription agencies have, or claim to have, ëcontactsí in stables and tend to tirelessly recommend runners from the second string stables that they have ëintimateí knowledge of. It may be that someone associated with the stable has genuinely communicated something first hand to the tipster but this ëinformationí is likely to be no more profound than a description of the horses breakfast and utterly irrelevant to the race in which it competes.

I operate what could be termed a Spread Betting system on the strength of tips given by a Northern based agency. Over a two month period the agency I monitored recommended over 200 horses and remarkably achieved a profit of 9% on starting prices. Apart from this fairly laudable profit, particularly seeing the vast number of the horses tipped, I was startled by the way in which the vast majority of their tips dramatically shortened in the market. It became evident that any horse they tipped, which was forecast as favourite, would tend to open up on course at significantly shorter odds than in the morning papers. In addition the majority of forecast second favourites would open on course as favourites and at lower prices than were forecast for the original favourite.

By buying the favourites market before one of the tipped favourites/ second favourites was running I appeared to be obtaining excellent value as their prices tended to take an enormous dive, and even at SP they still performed slightly better than their prices suggest.

Spread Betting on racing is very much at the cross-roads. Iím not convinced that the structure of the spreads is such that they will appeal to serious racing enthusiasts. **If one has analysed a race in great depth and wish to have a straightforward wager the advantages of fractional odds betting are generally clear.** If there is no increase in the number of performance indices on individual races, perhaps a culture will develop of playing the spread companies at their own game and making do with the markets on offer - though for this to happen a whole new body of knowledge will have to be developed.

'Value' in Spread Betting

6

Arbitrage opportunities set the pulses racing in serious spread enthusiasts

The concept of ëvalueí in traditional betting is now generally understood, though its application is a fairly subjective affair. Value betting simply refers to a situation where a bet should be struck when the true chances of an event happening are greater than those suggested by the odds. If the odds on Southampton are 4/1 (20%) to win their match at West Ham and, by whatever means, you assess that their ëtrueí chances of victory are nearer 25% (suggesting 3/1) then the 4/1 which you can obtain represents ëvalueí. The fact that Southampton doñít go on to actually win the game doesñít necessarily mean that you failed to obtain value in the price you took; similarly a winning bet doesñít automatically make it a value bet.

Over the long run, if you are consistently gaining a price of 4/1 on an event which is really only a 3/1 chance then, and although you can still only to expect to win one out of four of your bets, you must consistently be winning more than you are losing. The distinction between genuine ëvalueí and the more nebulous achievement of ëgetting a good priceí is somewhat hazy.

Many serious backers, particularly in racing, make their own book of odds the night before a race. If, following their interpretation of form, they highlight a horse that they feel might be undervalued in the betting market they might assign it a ëtargetí price of 4/1 that would make it an acceptable bet. Come the next day the horse opens at 5/1 and they get on immediately as their target criteria has been met. This is very much ësubjectiveí value seeking. Win or lose we can never really know whether the horse was ëgood valueí at 5/1. The difference between 3/1 (a 25% chance) and 5/1 (just under 17%) is comparatively small. When assessing a horses ëtrueí chances we are clearly not dealing in certainties.

In fact the only way to be sure a punter is obtaining value consistently is to observe whether they are winning more than losing - which leads us into a less than satisfactory circular argument.

True value can be identified, however, on a series of bets where it can be demonstrated conclusively that the price is wrong. Letís say you were offered 100/1 for finding a three draw treble on a coupon of Saturday matches. By looking at a reasonably large sample of matches it is easy to ascertain that the chances of any given match ending in a draw are about 26% (odds of 11/4). A treble at 11/4 works out to 53/1, substantially less than the odds on offer. If you place just one treble every week you will only win in roughly one out of 53 occasions but when it comes (at 100/1) it will be enough in the long run to see you get ahead and stay ahead.

An equivalent in Spread Betting would be if one was able to state categorically that the average winning margin in Grand Prix racing was 20 seconds. If one was to obtain a quote of 190 - 200 over a 16 race season it is clear that only a little over 12 seconds margin per race was being allowed for. Therefore you can be fairly certain that buying at 200 seconds represents tremendous value as the ëcorrectí spread should stand at more like 315 - 325, allowing 20 seconds winning margin per race. **This type of value is based on a structural pricing error and represents the 'holy grail' of bets for those looking for genuine value.**

Having grown up with the fractional odds system we tend to be mentally ësetí into thinking about the relative merits of competitors within the framework of fractional odds. In football matches we may have an instant feel about teams from their odds. A home team at 2/9 appears a near certainty, it might conjure up Manchester United versus a bottom half of the third division team. Odds of 4/5 might apply to Leeds at home Coventry; 6/4 both teams could be England v Italy.

If Holland are 32 - 35 on an index on their World Cup group where 40 is awarded to the winner, 20 for the runner up and 10 for third place it is not easy to assimilate quickly what this price indicates. It is as though we are being required to use a different currency. On this example the fact that points are being awarded for second and third places turns it into a form of each-way bet.

It is possible to compare prices between the spread firms if their system of assigning points is precisely the same. The main football and racing indices are, but many are not. When the first spreads were available on the 1998 World Cup groups the companies came up with different assignments of points. Take the previously mentioned Group E, where Holland were the seeded team as an example:

	Sporting Index	Hills
Holland	27 - 30	18 - 19.5
Belgium	18 - 21	10 - 11.5
Mexico	14 - 16	5 - 5.7
South Korea	6 - 8	4 - 5.5
	Win = 40	Win = 25
	Second = 20	Second = 10
	Third = 10	Third = 5
	Fourth = 0	Fourth = 0

If you fancied Holland to struggle in their group, which index would you be better off selling? A fairly straightforward calculation is to find the percentage of the points Holland's quote represents as a proportion of the total points on offer on the index. Taking the midpoint of the Sporting quote of 28.5 - this is 40.7% of the total of 70 points that are on offer: 40 + 20 + 10 = 70 points. In comparison Hills midpoint on Holland (18.75) represents 46.9% of the total of 40 points that are available to be won: 25 + 10 + 5 = 40 points. So on first inspection it would appear as though it is the Hill's index which rate Holland higher as the price accounts for a greater percentage of the total points on offer. Therefore, as a seller, it is preferable to sell Hill's index.

This can be confirmed by comparing the possible outcomes of selling both indices where the risk on each is the same. Choose a round figure, for instance £1000, and look at what happens when this sum is risked with both companies. A total loss of £1000 on the Sporting index would result if we sold at 27 for the ungainly sum of £76.92 (Holland would make-up at 40 if they won the group leaving us with a 13 point loss;

£1000 divided by 13 = £76.92). To risk the same £1000 with Hills our sell at 18 would be for £142.86 (We arrive at this figure by dividing £1000 by the maximum number of points that can be lost, seven; £1000 divided by 7 = 142.86).

The potential results of such sell wagers are as follows:

Holland's position	Hills	Sporting Index
First	lose £1000	lose £1000
Second	win £1143	win £538
Third	win £1857	win £1307
Forth	win £2571	win £2076

For the same risk of £1000 selling the Hills example at 18 would make you better off to the tune of £605 if Holland finished second, £550 if they were third, and £495 if they were last, as compared to going with Sporting Index. Therefore if one has the choice of a number of companies to make a trade with where different scoring systems are operated, it really does pay off to spend a few minutes calculating the exact figures.

Comparing prices offered by spread companies is the easiest form of assessing when a price is out of line from the true odds of the event occurring. Imagine a situation in which the spread companies offered the following supremacy quotes on an international football match between Scotland and Finland:

Hills	0.3 - 0.6
I.G	0.4 - 0.7
City	0.6 - 0.9
Sporting Index	0.4 - 0.7

There is a significant divergence between two firms, City and Hills. If there is value to be found it almost certainly must lie in selling City's quote of 0.6 or buying Hills quote of 0.6. As the City spread is the most different from the other three we might be tempted to conclude that a sell at 0.6 is the ëvalueí option. It is in these situations that it is a useful exercise to formulate your own target price before you set eyes on any spreads. If, in this example, you rated Scotlandís supremacy beforehand at 1.0 you could only be interested in buying Hills quote of 0.6. You can safely predict that the four companies will move their quotes into line by kick-off. Effectively this means that Cityís quote will be sold down to perhaps 0.4 - 0.7. It is highly unlikely that the other three firms will take the City lead and move upwards unless there is an unusual flurry of buying money.

Whilst comparing spread prices and fixed odds prices can cause major headaches, there is a simple method to check that they are roughly in line. This is to examine the rank order of the competitors. For example, the betting on the European championship might look like this:

Fixed odds		Spread quotes	
Germany	3/1	Germany	52 - 55
Italy	7/2	Italy	45 - 48
England	5/1	Holland	40 - 43
France	11/2	France	38 - 41
Holland	6/1	England	35 - 38
Norway	8/1	Croatia	32 - 35
Belgium	8/1	Belgium	30 - 33
Croatia	9/1	Norway	29 - 32

The actual scoring of the spread quotes is largely irrelevant in this example. The key is to compare the rank order of the quotes. Germany and Italy occupy ranks of one and two respectively in both tables. There are, however, significant differences in the relative ranking of England, who appear as third favourites in the fixed odds but only fifth favourites in the spread quotes, and Holland who are the fifth in the fixed odds but third on the spread. Any backer of England is probably getting a far better deal on the spreads than taking a fixed odds price, irrespective of the scoring mechanism used.

In updated markets you are being asked to potentially make two betting decisions as you are always given the option of closing a trade.

The concept of value is important in both decisions. Imagine you make a decision to sell cricket *Test Match Innings Runs*. Initially the spread stands at 320-340 for Australia. You sell at 320. Things go your way and the score at lunch is 68/3. The spread has slumped to 250 - 270 and you are in a position to buy back at 270 for a 50 point profit. You have appeared to have obtained value on your initial bet but is there a value component in buying back? The answer is quite possibly ënoí, even though it must be tempting to take your gains. The fundamental question is ëif the traders were wrong then, are they still wrong now?í If they are fundamentally overestimating Australiaís chances at every point then you should not consider buying back.

You sold when Australiaís quote was too high, if you buy back when it is still too high proportionally, you are effectively losing the value component of your initial bet - even though you won in financial terms you are, in a fashion, back where you started. I accept this proposition that you can ëloseí when you win might seem alien, but it must be stressed that value on the closing of a trade is equally as important as that when the bet is opened. If you close a trade you are effectively paying the spread company twice for privilege of trading on a single market. You are allowing them a theoretical margin on both the initial trade and the closure.

If you think the quote of 250 - 270 is still on the high side then you should hang on in there until it looks reasonable again. Say Australia go to 175 - 6 ; many of the initial buyers will have got out long ago and now the British will be engaged in a wave of hopeful selling, wanting to see the tail swept away for the loss of only a handful of runs. The spread stands at 210 - 220. Now you are not quite so sure. Some of the averages of the Aussie tail look quite reasonable - your sell bet was based on the fact that some of the top level batsmen had been very inconsistent of late. You now can imagine Shane Warne hitting a few to the boundary and a couple of irritatingly lengthy innings of attrition. Your estimate of the total is around the 235 mark. The value now in your opinion is at the buy end of the quote. You buy back at 220, taking a 100 point profit and watch happily as the Aussieís graft away for a total of 241.

If ëvalueí is at the heart of all betting decisions then it must take precedence over two familiar adages you frequently hear in relation to trading in general, and Spread Betting in particular...

    i) Ride your gains - Cut your losses
    ii) Always make sure your ëdowní side is less than
        your ëupí side.

I am suspicious of both of these oft quoted pearls of wisdom. For the first one to be true it seems to assume that once a market has started going one way then it will continue in that direction. If I was to sell winning distances at Newmarket at 12 and the first race made-up at three, sending the sell point of the spread to 13, what additional information is available to suggest that the losses are going to get worse? In fact if there was evidence that markets tend to continue going in the direction that they start to move, then surely a more useful adage would be to ëonly trade in the direction a market is goingí. This patently wonít work, therefore general advice to ëcut your lossesí is somewhat unhelpful. The value of the quote should be the only determining factor. If you believe that you have fundamentally read a market incorrectly and that the price you can close at underestimates the degree to which the event is going to go against your initial trading position, then by all means get out at that price.

It can be said, however, that you should only trade on your initial beliefs of a market. If West Ham are rated at 38 - 40 on an index of total points gained in the Premiership, you might look at their fixture list and see what you consider to be an ëeasyí first four games, in which they could pick up enough points to justify raising their spread. You buy heavily hoping to sell back at a profit after the 4th game. Things donít go the way you planned and the spread drops to 37-39 following the forth game. You are left with a considerable open position.

In these circumstances you might be advised to buy back at a loss simply as your initial theory has failed and you are left with an open position on a market you now have no opinion on. The value, if it was there in the first place, has now gone. However, if West Ham had won all of their first games the spread might rise to 48 - 50. The adage calls for you to ëride your gainsí but for you the bet is effectively over. The theory has worked, the quote now looks about right and you might be advised to sell back.

If your ëdowní side is greater than your ëupí side then this can mean no more than your potential gains are less than your potential losses - it tells you nothing about the merits of any particular bet. There is a reasonable argument in fractional betting that one should not back heavy odds-on favourites. This is primarily due to the proportion of your winnings which is taken up by the tax you pay on a bet.

If you place a £100 bet on a 1/4 shot your winning return is £125. The tax on your bet is £9 which will be lost if the bet fails. If you win you are throwing over a third of it away in tax. Since tax isnít levied on account holders in Spread Betting this is not an issue. The only factor in considering a bet is whether the chance of the event happening is considerably greater or less than the spread offered.

I have evidence to suggest that in certain situations a small upside may represent excellent value opportunities. Towards the end of an event that is traded in running, particularly football, it may well pay to sell the favourites, even though the rewards are comparatively small. Imagine, at the beginning of a match Chelseaís supremacy is quoted at 0.7 - 1.0 against Derby. The score remains 0-0 after 75 minutes play. The quote has dropped to 0.3 - 0.4. In this situation the spread companies will tend to have considerable liabilities on the buy-side of the favourites to the extent that they tend to be quite generous to those wishing to sell the favourites during the last phases of a game. In this example one would be tempted to conclude that a sell of supremacy was a large risk as the two most likely results are a draw or Chelsea victory by one goal. The former stands to make the seller 0.3 of a point whereas a Chelsea goal costs more than double at 0.7 of a point. Despite this discrepancy the value is almost certainly to be found with selling.

It has to be said that some markets are so one sided in their potential liabilities that only a trade in one particular direction looks appealing. If a quote on ëTime of the First Yellow Card in any gameí is offered on a major football tournament one might expect an offer of 120 - 140 seconds. This may correspond to the time of the first card in previous tournaments but clearly the potential for a freak result to occur on the buy side is much more evident than on the sell side where, even a vicious tackle on the man who receives the ball from the kick-off is only liable to lead to a make-up of five seconds. It is possible to conceive of an eventual make-up of more than 600. Where there is such an imbalance of liabilities most will shy away from leaving themselves open to the risk of massive losses in pursuit of modest gains, though there is an additional factor which needs to be considered. In a market where one end of the range of potential make up values is fixed and the other is virtually limitless, the spread tends to be adjusted towards the side with no limits.

If, in our example, the time of the first yellow card in the previous four tournaments had been 92 secís; 122 secís; 105 secís and 118 secís we can deduce that the spread of 120 - 140 is well above the average, which on the basis of these results, is just 109 secís. You would be inclined to think that sellers were on to a good thing as there had previously not been a make-up even approaching the buy point. However the spread is pitched on the high side to reflect the fact that, even though it may not have happened previously, there is a potential for a make-up massively above the spread.

Some markets are heavily skewed in terms of the range of make-ups. The total goals in a football match cannot be lower than zero but there is really no maximum. Manchester United could, one day, be involved in an 8 - 8 thriller with Liverpool.

The potential horrors that can be hiding in certain markets are illustrated by the ëbomb in the boxí analogy. Imagine you are faced with a wall of 1000 boxes, the contents of each are hidden under a lid. In every box, except one, there is a £10 note. In the remaining box there is a huge bomb set to explode when you open the lid. You are permitted to open any one box of your choosing every hour. Of course the chances are that you will ëwiní, (keep gaining £10) for a long period. Indeed, you could theoretically have 999 winners before you open the fatal box. The same sort of phenomena is evident in Spread Betting. You can happily keep making small profits on the same market for weeks on end when suddenly a catastrophic make up turns up which appears to be beyond belief.

Stop Losses/Wins

The imposition of limits on the amount of points that can be won or lost varies between firms and depends on the type of account you hold. In Test match cricket a Hills account holder has his wins and losses automatically capped at +/-200 runs from the trading point. An account holder with City Index is unlikely to have any stop loss/win imposed unless it has been specifically agreed prior to the trade taking place.

Stop losses/wins on first sight seem a blessing, especially bearing in mind the previous remarks about extreme make-ups, though if you examine their overall effect they can come to seem like an annoyance. These mechanisms are in place to keep both wins and losses within ëacceptableí limits to both parties. However limiting the range of potential make-ups works against the account holder. **Whilst stop wins/losses appear as though they might be some sort of concession to the backer, they are really very much in favour of the spread firm.** Stop loss/win mechanisms only apply to open ended markets, not to artificial indices.

A client who places a bet on a Test match *Total Runs* market can expect the make-up to be conceivably between 70 and 600 runs. Here the 20 point spread, say, 340-360 represents 3.7% of the total make-ups. However by limiting the potential make-ups to 200 each way the 20 point spread becomes 5% of the total possible make-ups. Thus the account holder with a stop loss/win mechanism ends up fighting against a higher margin in favour of the spread firm.

In many events ëmaximum make-upsí apply which tend to deaden the effect of extreme results. In racing spreads there is a general limit of 12 lengths placed on ëmatchí bets. If you have backed ëDawn Lightí to finish at least one length ahead of ëBlushing Brideí then the maximum you can win or lose by is 12 lengths. If your horse romps home 22 lengths in front you are only paid on a win of 12. If ëBlushing Brideí strides home 15 lengths in front of ëDawn Lightí you would be liable to a loss of 16 points if it wasnít for the fact that the stop loss has limited it to 12.

In looking at the values at which stop loss/wins are imposed (these are clearly stated in each firms literature) you could easily get the impression that coming up against them is exceedingly rare. I have found that I hit them on about 5% of all trades where they apply - enough to make me constantly aware of where they are set.

It must be noted that once you hit a stop win in-running the trade should always be closed. If you have sold Arsenal at a two goal supremacy against Southampton it is important to bear in mind that the stop loss/win is set at five either side of the trading point for this market. Southampton incredibly score four goals in 35 minutes and the spread now stands at Southampton supremacy of three - 3.3. You have absolutely no option but to immediately close the bet by selling Southamptonís supremacy at 3, thus giving you the maximum permitted profit of five goals. If Southampton go even further in the lead you do not make a penny. If Arsenal pull a goal back you can lose some of your gains.

The interesting area in this scenario is what your best course of action is should you be nearing your stop loss. When Southampton were 3-0 up the spread might have been 2 - 2.3 in favour of Southampton. At this point there is a cap on any improvement in Southamptonís supremacy which is potentially just a few minutes away. Theoretically it could be argued that you should close the bet unless you honestly think that the price is incorrect and still favours Arsenal too much; in which case you have every right to keep the trade going and hope that Southampton score again and hit your stop win.

Maximum make- ups and Stop losses/wins are valuable when your trade has its loss potential limited but where there is no effect on your upside. If one was to buy ëTime of the Fastest Goalí in the European Championships any stop loss is likely only to come into effect on the buy side and could provide an effective barrier to losses spiralling

Arbitrage

A rbitrage is a term imported from financial trading which is applicable to Spread Betting. In a trading sense it refers to the practice of taking advantage of differential prices of the same commodity on different exchanges and currencies. Nick Leeson, the Barings trader whose dealings helped cause the collapse of the merchant bank was engaged in these perfectly legitimate deals before he started writing open positions with such catastrophic consequences.

Imagine, there is a live TV game where Hills have given a quote of 31 - 34 on the shirt numbers worn by the goal scorers in the game. City Index along with most of the other firms have gone 36 - 39. If you had an account with both you could sell 36 with City Index and buy 34 with Hills. If the make-up was 28 you would lose six points on the Hills trade but gain eight points on the City Index trade giving you an overall profit of two points. The make-up is immaterial. The fact that you have bought at two points lower than you have sold has locked in the profit.

Arbitrage opportunities set the pulses racing in serious spread enthusiasts and their existences are eagerly highlighted in the press. If you can strike both the trades then you should be congratulated for a excellent 'mini coup'. There are, however, a number of words of warning before taking such a plunge.

To operate an arbitrage successfully you need a fairly substantial credit rating. To make just £200 on your deal you will need to take strike two trades at £100 a point. You are likely to end up owing one of the companies a fairly substantial sum. They are not to know that you are about to make an even larger gain with another company so you will have to demonstrate that you are in a position of being able to repay possibly up to £5000 losses. Remember this is simply to make £200. The nightmare scenario in attempting an arbitrage is that one or both companies will suddenly move their prices back into line and/or that one refuses you the bet to its full amount because of insufficient credit. Just because youíve successfully obtained a sell with City Index at 36 doesnít mean you can necessarily execute the trade with Hills to buy at 34.

Meltdown becomes more likely when you are refused the second trade and decide to leave your £100 a point sell trade open. The game inevitably is a 0-0 draw, the make up zero, you get stung for a bill for £3600 and Spread Betting has decidedly lost its allure.

Having tried to put you off there are a number of things you can do to make arbitrage relatively risk free and profitable. If one company is obviously out of line with the rest then it makes sense to take their price before moving on to the other companies with the ëstandardí price. If you want to avoid disappointment then it is important you seek out arbitrage opportunities for yourself. You cannot rely on any that are reported in the racing press. If at 10 am you read in *The Racing Post* that there is a 3 point ëarbí (as they are increasingly terming it) then by the time you get on the phone the companies will almost certainly have bought their prices into line.

Arbitrage opportunities have a tendency to turn up more in some markets rather than others. Where a market is worked out using a standard mathematical formula (such as horse racing *Double Card Numbers*) you can generally expect all the companies to have done their sums in the same way and arrive at pretty much the same quote. Where there is a genuine element of subjective assessment going on there are more likely to be a variety of different factors that the spread firms are taking account of, and hence they are more likely to come up with divergent quotes.

In my experience the market which seems to cause the greatest disagreements between companies is that which is offered on *Total Goals Homes/Aways Supremacy* in football. This is a market run by all the spread companies on groups of games occurring at the same time. You might see a quote on Premier (8) 2.5 - 3.5. On the eight Premiership games happening that afternoon you are being asked to predict whether the aggregate of goals scored by home teams will be more than 3.5 or less than 2.5 than the aggregate goals of away teams. These quotes regularly produce some spectacular arbitrage opportunities. The markets are generally published on Teletext on Wednesday night (for the following Saturdayís games) with the first opportunity to trade on Thursday morning.

The reason why they are so variable is the fact that they are an aggregate of the companies quotes on the goals supremacy markets for each of the matches individually. Companies tend to have slightly different ëpoliciesí regarding the pricing up of football supremacy. For instance, as on their fixed odds coupons, Hills tend to be slightly more generous with their prices on away teams i.e. high home team supremacy. On the spreads slight differences one way or the other add up through the individual games and by the time a homes/aways supremacy rating is arrived at for groups of games some large price differences start occurring.

What is particularly attractive about them is the fact that they are rarely reported in the racing press leading to the prices being held over for long periods. I have occasionally seen arbitrage positions still merrily being offered on Friday morning for this market.

In football the *Shirt Number* and *Disciplinary* markets also tend to be subject to a few arbitrage opportunities. A few opportunities exist in the overall supremacy markets, particularly in matches where British teams are playing foreign opposition whose merits might be the subject of disagreements amongst the firms.

7 Market Focus: Cricket

I have found that the cricket spreads have provided me with excellent profits. And I would venture that for any individual who follows the game seriously, the potential to get ahead and stay ahead of the spread firms is high.

The ponderous nature of cricket, especially at Test match level, is not every persons idea of the peak of sporting drama. Yet the pace of a match lends itself to Spread Betting. Even for those who are not great followers of the game, a spread bet on the total runs made in an innings can hardly be matched for excitement value. Betting in running on other sports can be a fraught activity. With cricket and its convenient breaks between overs, one can plan ahead, calculate run rates, compare the quotes of competing spread firms, and only strike a bet when 100% confident.

The drawback of the sportís leisurely pace is that following a cricket bet becomes something of a time consuming activity. Place a bet a few minutes before the opening of a Test innings at 10.50am on a Saturday morning and strong nerves are needed to tear yourself away from the coverage long enough to put the kettle on, let alone go out. If the bet is left to run the innings is likely to last through the seven hours of the dayís play and drift on into the next. **The potential for Spread Betting to become addictive and disruptive to the normal patterns of everyday life is nowhere more evident than the cricket spreads.**

Having issued that health warning, I have found that the cricket spreads have provided me with excellent profits. And I would venture that for any individual who follows the game seriously, the potential to get ahead and stay ahead of the spread firms is high.

For many there is no need to look beyond betting in running on the *Total Innings Runs* market-though there are a host of bets to be had on subsidiary markets with varying degrees of attraction. Test match series see a flurry of markets based on individuals batting and bowling performances. For example, Brian Lara may be quoted at 370 - 390 runs during an entire six match Test series. To achieve this total you could say that he needs to score 32.5 runs in each of 12 innings. There is, however, the paradox that a good batting performance in the first innings of a Test makes it less likely that his side will need to bat again for any long period. You can find yourself cheering his contribution and yet hoping that the rest of the side is dismissed fairly cheaply (though not so cheaply that he runs out of partners), thus making a second innings, and an opportunity to score further runs, more likely. This type of situation, where it is not absolutely clear where your loyalties lie is rather uncomfortable and does not make a sporting event particularly pleasant viewing. An individualís performance in a Test series is updated after every Test. But as a buyer you always risk the chances of your man getting injured between Tests.

Such a fate befell Darren Gough whilst playing for Yorkshire between Test match duties for England in their last home series against Australia. If you happen to be at a county ground when a Test player falls to the ground holding their ankle then there is nothing to stop you getting on the phone and selling their Test match performance quote in the hope that they will be injured and unable to play. In offering long term markets on players performances the spread companies open themselves to such trading, though in terms of ë**ungentlemanly conduct**í it ranks fairly high.

About one in ten players quoted on performance indices at the start of a Test series do not make it to the end, whether through injury or as a result of being dropped from the team for poor performances. This fact alone is enough to ensure that I tend to instantly dismiss any thoughts of buying a *Players Performance Index*.

The fundamental cricket spread is the quote on *Total Innings Runs*. This is generally offered about 10 minutes before the start of play. If, in a Test match, England are batting on a fine day the quote may be expected to start at 320-340. There is every likelihood that the companiesí quotes will differ, often substantially so. In those 10 minutes there can be a large volume of trading and the price may fluctuate considerably. When trading is mostly in one direction the spread may move as much as +/- 30 runs, so it is conceivable that one can move into a profit situation in the space of less than 10 minutes and without a ball being bowled.

Cricket is perhaps the most weather sensitive sport of them all. Firstly, in terms of the overall result - rain means more suspensions of play and a greater likelihood of a draw in Test matches played over five days. In addition, the weather leading up to and during a match determines how the ball reacts through the air and when it hits the playing surface. The difference the state of the pitch makes to the potential overall score in an innings is huge. On a flat surface with dry/hot conditions and no interruptions a Test innings of 500 puts the team batting first in a good position. On a day where there is significant cloud cover and an uneven pitch the ball may turn and swing erratically, so that a score of 230 looks more than reasonable.

Many choosing to have a spread bet on an innings wait to hear the ëpitch reportí that is broadcast about five minutes before the opening play. This tactic is fine, though a pitch report which is not in keeping with the general conditions is going to affect the spread. So if there is any hint of a poor pitch itís best not to hang around too much - the most frustrating position to be caught in is dithering over selling when the pitch is clearly going to play worse than expected. Waiting for a few overs, only to see two wickets fall and the quote drop is one of those unfortunate ëif onlyí situations.

As play progresses the spread changes to reflect the state of the game. As batsmen set themselves and start knocking the ball to the boundary the spread will climb. Should a wicket fall the spread will undergo a significant collapse immediately. The extent of this lowering of the spread will be largely determined by the quality of the batsmen lost. Individual batsmen runs can be wagered on separately so, if Nick Knight opens the England batting with Alec Stewart, there will be three separate quotes in running which might look like this:

Knight Runs	40 - 43
Stewart Runs	38 - 41
England Innings	320 - 340

The quotes on individual batsmen are essentially a mix of the individuals Test match average overlaid on other relevant factors i.e. the state of the pitch and strength of the opposition. In the above example Knight is ëexpectedí to contribute just over 40 runs. If he is out without scoring England have ëlostí his runs and therefore one might expect the quote on the *Total Innings Runs* to decrease by 40. If ,on the other hand, he makes 40 runs by lunch his individual spread may rise to 78 - 81. Again, should he be out then the difference between his ëexpectedí runs (the midpoint of the current spread) and his actual runs will be subtracted from the Total Innings spread.

A bet on individual batsmen runs is guaranteed to set the heart racing. As a buyer, every ball bowled until the batsmen reaches the desired number of runs is a potential wipe-out. As a seller the spread moves upwards consistently and leaves your sell point far behind, which does little for morale. In general there is little enthusiasm for selling batting performances as the liability on such a bet appears enormous. A seller of Stewartís runs at 38 can only look forward to a potential win of 38 points if he is dismissed without scoring, but the consequences of a century or even double century are appalling. However, this general perception can aid the seller who is likely to be in a small minority.

Initial prices tend to be slightly higher than that which is statistically justified. The fact that so many are put off from selling means that, in my experience, there appears to be very little value to be found in buying either individual *Batsmen Runs* or indeed *Total Innings Runs*. Indeed, traders have gone on record as stating that, on a good pitch, there is an endless stream of buyers.

A popular technique seems to be to wait for a couple of overs to see how the pitch is playing. However, I have been somewhat surprised that most of the market moves seem to happen just before the start of play and not following the first few deliveries. On a number of occasions I have managed to sell the *Total Innings Runs* at the opening quote even though it is obvious to viewers and TV commentators that the ball is moving more than expected.

The key to the general overestimates that gamblers make in judging the number of runs a team is likely to make may stem from their misjudgement of the effect of a couple of wickets falling quickly. One of my favoured sell points is when teams make a reasonable start, perhaps reaching a total of 100 for the loss of two wickets. It is easy to imagine that the batting team might lose another couple of wickets in reaching 200, and then with a bit of a flourish from the tail, end up with a score in the mid 300ís. Whilst not wishing to suggest any rigid rules of how innings progress I am constantly struck by how fast a seemingly good start deteriorates into a poor position. A score of 100 for 2 becomes 130 - 5 in the space of a few overs and suddenly the tail end batsmen are at the crease. Keeping a close eye on the spreads for the three most recent England Test series, there were precious few occasions when the spread wasnít consistently on the high side.

In deciding whether to have a bet I try to make an estimate of the number of runs I think a team will reach without knowing the quote offered. Only having reached an ëindependentí conclusion would I see if the spread is out of line with my thinking. It is generally the case that the quote is roughly in line or higher than the figure I have in mind. If it is higher by 30 or more I would generally have a sell bet immediately.

The difficulties come if you have set yourself up to have a bet and then the companies essentially agree with your estimate. This disappointment is present with many betting situations but is particularly relevant to cricket. If you have an opportunity to watch an event, whether it be live or on TV, it is unfortunate to find that, in all honesty, there doesnít seem to be a decent bet to be had. It is in this situation that bets are struck which are later regretted.

The quote moves in response to the state of play. If one was to agree with the initial quote of, for example, 320 - 340 and sit back and watch the first few overs, the batting team may reach 20 without loss. A check on the quote now invariably will see it rise to 340 - 360. The new quote is simply the opening figure plus the number of runs that the batsmen have achieved. This is essentially the standard formula by which the firms move the quotes, though if the batting side are having a particularly testing time the quote may stay resolutely where it started, or even lower.

Assuming that play is progressing ënormallyí, you now have an opportunity to sell at a price 20 runs higher than when the innings opened, even though little has happened on the field of play to suggest that the initial quote was too low. I would suggest that, in order to reach the estimated total (midpoint 330 - about an average first innings) the openers will have to put on an ëaverageí first wicket stand. If we accept that this is around 40 then the fact that they have attained 20 without loss is insufficient to demonstrate that they are going to exceed that score before the first wicket falls, which surely is implied by the overall spread rising by 20.

In response to this tendency for the spread to rise, as I see it, somewhat too quickly, my other favoured sell point is when the innings is in the low 20ís without the loss of a wicket. This particularly holds if scoring is slow. In the cases where the batsmen are putting on runs very quickly I prefer to hang on until there is any sign of the runs drying up - possibly a maiden by a new bowler, and then sell.

The fact that wickets fall during an innings, making the spread collapse suddenly, complicates the essential nature-of-the-problem of how quickly a *Total Innings Runs* spread should rise. To look into the mechanics of it closer it is better to examine this with reference to the spread on individual batsmen runs. For example, the spread on Alec Stewartís runs is 39 - 42 when he first comes into bat. He goes on to make 10 runs, unbeaten. In the new circumstances what should be the revised estimate of the number of runs he will make?

There are a variety of different opinions on this conundrum. A surprising number of people will argue that the original estimate of 40 should remain unchanged. This is false, as his average score (on which the spread is based on) includes a number of occasions when he was dismissed for under 10 runs; he has avoided this fate on this occasion so the current estimate must be higher than his average.

The opposite position is the one adopted by the spread companies which is to add the total runs already achieved to the estimate. So, in the case of the above example Alec Stewartís new runs spread would be expected to rise to 49 - 52. This makes strict mathematical sense in that any solution which relies on the gap between the runs scored and the estimate getting closer falls into the trap that at some point the runs achieved ëcatches upí with the spread. Nevertheless, I am not totally convinced that a batmen who reaches 0.25 of his average score can be deemed to be on target for scoring a total that is 1.25 of his average.

For readers not inclined to examine this in more detail, and I canít honestly say I blame you. I would suggest simply that you look for evidence that a batsmen is faltering, either scoring very slowly or giving away half chances, and sell with confidence. Whilst the spectre of a batsmen going on to achieve a double century tends to awkwardly spring to mind in these situations, I feel that there are generally enough clues pointing to a wicket about to fall to make this a reasonably safe tactic.

A general spread on the result of a Test match is usually based on a simple 25 : 10 : 0 index where 25 is awarded for the win and 10 for the draw. So coming into the last day of a Test match you might see the following quotes:

England	20 - 22
Pakistan	3 - 5

Here England are clearly on top, perhaps needing another 90 runs to secure victory with seven wickets remaining. The 10 points awarded for the draw complicate matters somewhat. There are three points between Englandís buy point and the 25 points they are awarded for winning. And similarly three points between Pakistanís sell point and the zero they receive for losing. So if you are absolutely sure that England will knock off the runs required with little trouble it doesnít matter whether you sell Pakistan or buy England. However anyone tempted to believe that Pakistan can bowl England out, or that rain will stop the batsmen from reaching the target, must sell England as the potential profit is 10 points for the draw and 20 should Pakistan win. This compares to the position of a Pakistan buyer who makes just five for the draw and 20 for the win. Here, the fact that the draw is not awarded exactly half the points allocated for the win means a momentís careful thought is required when going in on this market.

In limited overs games the actual result takes on more significance; here the companies differ in their presentation of markets on the overall result. Generally there is a supremacy quote whereby one point is awarded for every run won by and 10 points for every wicket won by.

Remember that the side batting first can only win by runs, the side batting second only by wickets.

One day cricket is essentially all about run rates. If anything, on studying the spreads for one day games, I tend to believe we are inclined to underestimate the number of runs which can be scored per over, especially at the end of the innings. This makes me tempted to look at buying a sideís runs; very much the opposite of the position in Test matches where there is an inclination to overestimate the total score achievable.

Take an example where Kent are 132 for 2 after the 30th over of a 50 over match. Their current run rate is 132 divided by 30 = 4.4 per over. One could estimate that they are capable of achieving an increased run rate of five per over for the remainder of the innings. This would leave them with an estimated total of 232. In fact a more realistic estimate is reached by taking into account a small number of high scoring overs towards the end of an innings. In their remaining overs Kent might score;

> 4 in all of 7 overs
> 5 in all of 6 overs
> 8 in all of 5 overs, and
> 12 in only 2 overs,

In a large majority of the overs remaining they donít score at over five per over. This can easily lead to the impression that their run rate isnít more than five per over. The effect of the small number of big scoring overs on the total is vast. In the above example Kent would finish their innings with a total of 254, even though one might get an impression that their run rate was ëon targetí for a significantly lower total. This is related to the illusion that is evident when assessing *Winning Distances* in racing - an average (in this case run rates) is increased substantially by ëfreakí scores, though it is easy to overlook their significance because they happen infrequently.

The shape of one day cricket has been changed considerably since the introduction of fielding restrictions in the first 15 overs of the innings. This gives the batting side an opportunity to strike some quick runs, and indeed the run rates at which some innings start are fearful.

A score of 50 off the first five overs is perfectly within the realms of possibilities and some opening batsmen have gained a reputation for making hay at the beginning of the innings. Most of the companies are now offering quotes on *First 15 Over Runs* - for British county games you can expect a quote of around 60 - 65.

I tend to find that the buy side, if anything, offers greater potential - it is just a question of picking out those opening batsmen with aggressive intent. One should not underestimate the degree to which the end of fielding restrictions can significantly blunt the scoring power of the batsmen. If you think the overall innings runs spread is on the high side you may get excellent value in selling just after the first 15 overs.

Of all betting sports, cricket is the one which really requires you to look beyond the immediate situation of the match. If the ball is flying to the boundary, just about all your fellow account holders will be looking to get on the side of the batting team. This is the best reason in the world to be aware of the possibilities of selling total runs. If wickets start falling everyone else will be imagining the potential for a total collapse, in which case you should be concentrating on the chances of a good partnership and partial recovery.

8 Market Focus: Greyhounds

The multi-traps index ranks as perhaps the most heavily geared and violently fluctuating market of any account holders regularly come across.

Greyhound racing has a decidedly mixed image. On the one hand betting shop turnover figures demonstrate that revenue on the dogs is at its highest on days when there are only one or two poor quality horse racing meetings. This indicates that it is simply a means of keeping the hardened betting shop regulars contributing to the coffers until something better comes along. UK dog tracks have a reputation as seedy and uninspiring environments to spend an afternoon and their devotees are advancing in age, leading many in the bookmaking industry to forecast a long term decline in its importance.

Despite this impression, greyhound racing contributes 20% of betting shop turnover, completely dwarfing football turnover at 4%- and football is generally heralded as the major growth area in gambling revenue. The dogs account for about 6% of spread bets, a very respectable proportion considering there are generally only one or two indices a day and following the results may be a question of aimlessly watching Ceefax pages tick over.

When I embarked on Spread Betting I confess to having virtually no interest in the dogs. The reason why I decided to investigate it further was the way in which the spread firms had designed their index for meetings. The *Multi-Traps Index* (or ëmulti-muttsí as Hills unromantically term it) ranks as perhaps the most heavily geared and violently fluctuating market of any account holders regularly come across. The fact that one can experience such a betting rollercoaster ride on events that rank, in fairness, fairly low in terms of sporting prestige, makes it peculiarly attractive. The prize money for a winning owner in a BAGS race averages around £60. Even on absolute minimum Spread Betting stakes it is very easy to win or lose that figure on every race. Hence a ësmallí stakes gambler tends to have more of a financial interest in the results than the participants; not a situation that arises in, for instance, Formula One racing, or just about any other sport.

Multi-Traps indices are published around 30 minutes before the start of afternoon racing on weekdays and morning racing on Saturdays. The index is on the total of the multiplied forecast numbers per race. Therefore if trap 6 beats trap 5 (6x5) the race make-up is 30. If 3 beats 1 (3x1) the race make-up is three. There are generally 12 races in an afternoon BAGS meeting, though this can rise to 13 and 14 occasionally. Eight race cards are featured on Saturday morning. With a 12 race card the theoretical range of overall make-ups is huge. In the event of traps 1 and 2 occupying the forecast positions in every race the twelve race total would be 24 (12x2). Should 6 and 5 monopolise the forecast positions the make-up will end up at a massive 360. This leaves a total range of 336, and anything but a dull market.

Much of the betting speculation surrounding dog racing has little to do with the merits of the individual runners. There are legions of punters who bet solely on trap numbers, perceiving that the trap a dog runs from has a vital importance in determining the outcome. Hence, in bookmakers every day, a significant proportion of all dog bets are ëthrough the cardí forecasts; traps 1 and 2 Reverse Forecast for Wimbledon, 5 and 6 for Hove etc.

There is firm evidence that this strategy is based on fact, even though its proponents who hammer away on a daily basis are likely to make a substantial level stakes loss, despite bumper payouts once in a while.

In general terms the chances of a race being won by any particular trap number must be 16.67% (100 divided by the 6 traps).

Actual percentage wins of individual trap numbers
Sample: 10,900 races at 7 tracks

Trap 1	Trap 2	Trap 3	Trap 4	Trap 5	Trap 6
18.5%	16.4%	15.6%	15.4%	16.1%	18.0%

The above table demonstrates that traps 1 and 6 have a clear advantage, being significantly higher than the mean. The middle traps (3 and 4) suffer a disadvantage. The percentages may not look dramatically different but in Spread Betting terms they can mean a great deal. When multiplying forecast trap numbers together, as the spread demands, differences become magnified enormously.

The possible make-ups of an individual race display some interesting characteristics. There are 15 possible:

1 and 2 m/u 2	2 and 3 m/u 6	3 and 4 m/u 12	4 and 5 m/u 20	5 and 6 m/u 30
1 and 3 m/u 3	2 and 4 m/u 8	3 and 5 m/u 15	4 and 6 m/u 24	
1 and 4 m/u 4	2 and 5 m/u 10	3 and 6 m/u 18		
1 and 5 m/u 5	2 and 6 m/u 12			
1 and 6 m/u 6				

The mean make-up is 11.66. This must be the starting point for the firms when offering quotes. Multiplying this by the 12 races gives 140, which is somewhere near the midpoint of opening quotes. However the arithmetic mean doesnít tell the whole story. Of the 30 possible forecasts, sixteen make-up below the mean and only fourteen above it, and four of those (ë2 and 6í reversed and ë3 and 4í reversed) are within 0.34 of the mean. The distribution of possible make-ups is skewed by the multiplying them together. This is another example of the ëbomb in the boxí syndrome described previously. If you are a seller you can happily watch a majority of races come down in your favour but fear a *freak* ë6 and 5í that is potentially disastrous. As a buyer you have fewer chances of profiting but when they come along they are worth waiting for.

There are good reasons why traps 1 and 6 perform better than average. Trap 1, on the inside, simply has less distance to travel; trap 6 tends to avoid the cut up ground on the inside, particularly as the meeting progresses. I have tested this theory out and, indeed, there is a very slight tendency for the outside traps to ëimproveí over the course of the meeting (On a sample of 400 meetings the forecast numbers multiplied together was 4% higher in the last four races of a meeting than the first four). Perhaps most significant is the fact that the outside runners cannot be bumped from both sides as is the case with traps 2, 3, 4 and 5. Watch a few dog races in progress and it soon becomes obvious that those in the middle traps tends to get flung around more on the bends, to the extent that one good bash from either side can put the dog out of the race immediately. British tracks are not of a uniform design - some are particularly tight, particularly Crayford.

There are essentially two considerations to make in assessing the likely make-up of a dog meeting:

a) The mean make-up for previous meetings at the track.
b) The traps in which the favourites for the meeting are running.

Particular track biases form the basis for the hardened betting shop regulars that doggedly pursue forecasts through the card. What follows is an attempt at a definitive list of mean make-ups for the tracks on which spread markets are generally based. The figures are derived from a sample of more than 15,000 races though it should be noted that, to give the largest possible sample, the races analysed include all the meetings at a particular track, including those in the evening. They are therefore not limited to the actual BAGS races on which spread markets are offered.

Ranked mean make-ups for principal greyhound tracks

	Mean make-up per race	Mean make-up per 12 race card
Perry Bar	12.682	152.0
Hove	12.228	146.7
Sheffield	12.092	145.1
Hall Green	11.455	138.8
Monmore	11.459	137.5
Crayford	11.356	136.3
Sunderland	11.422	137.1
Bristol	11.085	133.0
Wimbledon	10.875	130.5
Walthamstow	10.705	128.5

Of course the deviation from the presented means is considerable. Though I have yet to see a market make-up outside the range of the 100 stop loss that generally applies,(roughly speaking, lower than 35 or higher than 240), one can expect around 7% of the make-ups to fall under 100 and a similar percentage over 175. I have found that only 33% of meetings make-up to within 10 points either way of the opening quotes.

Of those listed I tend to leave Hove alone; though it has the highest frequency of trap 6 wins, it is well below average for 4ís and 5ís. As a buyer you cannot sit back happy in the knowledge that plenty of 6ís should romp home if there are no other higher numbers coming in second place to multiply it by. The result of this is that Hove is the most volatile track of the lot. The last two make-ups at the time of writing were 236 and 92.

Perry Bar tops the list on account of having high 6ís, high 5ís, and the lowest 1ís and 2ís. This combination gives it a mean make-up of 152. Opening quotes for Perry Bar meetings rarely push over the 139-144 mark and as such this makes an attractive buy. Generally I tend to **favour selling the tracks with lower mean make-ups** and, as the above table clearly illustrates, Wimbledon and Walthamstow particularly fit the bill. Wimbledon has the highest percentage of 1 wins of all the featured tracks, though weighs in with second highest 6ís. Walthamstow is the perfect sellers track with high 1ís and 2ís and very low 5ís and 6ís. A mean make-up figure of 128 puts it below virtually all opening quotes which tend to start off in the region of 136-141.

Having established the mean make-ups per track the other consideration that has to be ëlayeredí onto this information is the strengths of the individual dogs running from each trap. Taking a single race as an example, imagine that traps 6 and 5 are joint favourites (both 6/4), with the other tracks nowhere in betting. The track make-up average per race is low at 11.55. How should we go about estimating the make-up for this particular race. The most favoured make-up must be 30 (6 beating 5 or vice versa) but how far should the estimate climb towards 30 from its track mean of 11.55?

To begin to answer this question we have to plunge into assessment of the performances of favourites. Overall the performance of greyhound favourites is very poor. In 500 races that I examined a pound on each favourite would have made a loss of 32%. In fact a pound on all the other traps bar the favourite produced a better result, a loss of 23%. We have already established that in a race where all the runners were of

equal ability any individual dog should have a 16.67% chance of winning. The chance of it finishing second must also be 16.67%. Add these
together (33.34) and you get the chance of any one dog finishing in the
first two (which after all is what we are interested in for spread purposes). The actual percentage of favourites finishing in the top two is
47% (higher, though not spectacularly so, than the average). It should
then follow that if a high proportion of the favourites are coming out of
trap 6 the make-ups for each race should be higher than the mean of
11.66. This is because there should be more 6ís in the first two home
and six multiplied with any other trap number except one will give a
race make-up of over the 11.66 mean.

I have gone on to look at the relationship between paperís forecasts
and final make-ups. For every BAGS meeting *The Racing Post* makes
a forecast prediction for each race. I have used these forecasts as the
basis of the analysis (rather than first and second favourites) as it neatly
avoids the difficulties of runners predicted to go off at the same price.

For example, imagine that a paper predicts the following results for a
12 race card at Wimbledon:

First	2	5	3	1	6	6	4	5	2	4	6	5
Second	5	4	6	3	4	5	1	6	4	5	4	4

If these really turned out to be the results the make-up will end up
as 211. Here the favourites are running from higher trap numbers
than a normal distribution. The opening spread is 147-152. Tempted
to buy? The only way of seeing how much relationship there is
between the predictions and the actual make-ups is to look at a
large sample of results.

Taking 400 meetings I performed a statistical test termed a
ëco-efficient of correlationí between the make-ups that were implied by the tipsters selections and the actual make-ups. The test
comes up with a measure of the relationship between the two sets
of figures; a precise positive relationship (i.e. the two sets of data
are identical) will produce an ëanswerí of one, whereas if their is
no relationship between them (totally random) the answer is zero.

My data produced a correlation of 0.22 (you could think of this as being 22% better than totally random).

This is pretty much negligible, suggesting that the presence of favourites in specific traps has little bearing on the eventual make-up.

However, I doubt whether that is how other backers see it; they will be looking at the possibility of getting on the side of favourites by buying, if for instance a disproportionate number of favourites are running from high trap numbers. In situations where there the quote is moving ëtowardsí the favourites it may well pay to go in the other direction.

The best companies at present to have an account with for greyhound markets are Hills and Sporting Index as they offer quotes on both the daily midweek BAGS meetings whereas other companies only offer one. There is frequently a worthwhile difference in the various quotes. The situation where one companyís sell price is the same as anotherís buy price is quite common.

There is perhaps one other variable that is worth noting - inevitably, that of the weather. This was brought home to me one particular Wednesday afternoon when the quote for a meeting at Hove began to shoot up before racing from 140-145 to 155-160. With the heavens opening on the south coast track all the money started coming in on the outside trap numbers (as it was presumed that these would avoid sloshing around the tighter turns that had to be negotiated by the inside traps). The price for a dog in trap 6 may have been 4/1 in the morning paper but just before the off this generally might have shrunk to around the 6/5 favourite mark. The meeting ended up making up to 185, considerably higher than the mean for Hove. It was striking that the spread did not start to move until close to the time of the first race when SIS pictures are broadcast from the track; so it would appear that, as with so many spreads across many sports, it pays to know precisely what the weather is doing at the venue before pictures are broadcast.

9 The Quest for Information

If you sense a weight of ill-informed opinion going in one particular direction, quietly take out a spread position going the opposite way

Letís be realistic; most of us donít spend our Saturdays in a private box at Cheltenham followed by dinner with Henry Cecil to discuss the audacious ëstrokeí planned for Newton Abbott on Wednesday, returning home to find an anonymous soul has left a message on the answerphone to the effect that Everton will be fielding their youth squad in their FA Cup replay. In reality we watch *Match of the Day*, read the back pages of national newspapers and perhaps chip into conversations with hardened betting shop regulars which only occasionally reach levels above, ìIíve got a strong feeling about this oneî.

There are a number of key elements in the search for good information relating to spread markets, the most glamorous of which is to try and glean some breaking news that the spread companies have not had a chance to take into account when compiling their markets. There are undoubtedly a successful minority of account holders who pursue this tactic tirelessly as, unlike fixed odds betting, the ability to back competitors to do badly means that any hint that a footballer is injured or a snooker player has snapped their favourite cue can often be seized upon to make instant profits without the usual worry of having to analyse the event itself.

The role the general media play in interpreting sporting events is crucial to the publicís perception. Spread account holders definitely react to what they see and read - it is up to you how much faith you put in reports; are they just part of the general public relations hype or is there a genuinely worthwhile information to be gleaned? Just prior to the beginning of the 1997/98 football season the BBC news ran an item on its on newly promoted Barnsley, who had their first season in the Premiership to look forward to. There was a general feeling that Barnsley would struggle to avoid finishing last in the table, and whilst this was acknowledged in the report it mainly concentrated on the bullishness and optimism of players and supporters suggesting that a top half of the table finish was by no means out of the question. That afternoon following a couple of airings of the report Barnsleyís spread on the Total Premiership Points rose by two points (remember this is before a ball was kicked of the season). This readjustment must surely have been based on the upbeat TV coverage.

Similarly, prior to the 1998 World Cup there had been a FIFA directive to tournament referees that certain types of tackles (mainly tackles from behind), previously punishable by a yellow card, would be liable to a red card. When the red cards market opened it stood at 18 - 21 . As the media machine rolled into action in the final run-up the TV companies and national press ran the story that British referee Paul Durkin had been training with the England squad and had issued warnings that players from all the competing nations could find themselves in trouble with the new directive - hinting that red cards could be handed out very liberally. In a sense he was adding no new information but his comments caused the spread firms to raise the index to a high of 44 - 47 shortly after the story broke.

On this sort of occasion there are only two points to trade. If you were actually privy to the knowledge that Mr Durkin was about to make the statement then that is clearly the time to get in with a buy. If you essentially believed its just another story churned out in a desperate attempt to fill the back pages until something more interesting comes along, then you would judge when the story has run its course and execute a sell when the market hit its peak.

General media coverage of sport (with the possible exception of racing, where betting is inextricably linked with the contests) avoids any serious attempts at analysing events from the betting angle. Too often the media is interested in sterile interviews with participants and the frequently shallow interventions of pundits. How often are we forced to hear yet another jockey or trainer earnestly intone that his mount should, ìget a good rideî or the hope of a football manager that, ìwe are capable of getting the right resultî. The pundits themselves rarely are particularly enlightening from the betting angle. If Arsenal are

4/11 favourites to win a match televised live we donít need to be told that, ìyou must consider Arsenal to be favourites but of course strange things happen in footballî.

There are a few notable exceptions to this; pundits who appear to be making comments that go against what one is seeing before oneís own eyes, but who tend to predict events correctly. In this rare category Geoff Boycott must take a bow. When other pundits are predicting that a score of less than 300 must be considered disappointing he attracts scorn by venturing that ë160 might seem a good score on this pitchí. It is only when the score reaches 155 for 9 that one makes a mental note to be alert in future for his crystal ball gazing.

For football, the BBCís Alan Hanson also has a rather useful habit of pronouncing a team basically unsound even if they have just beaten opposition, on the face of it, quite convincingly. This is just the sort of mind set that is useful for account holders to develop. It is much more beneficial to see a competitor/team get a good result and to be able to find reasons why their results may not be so good in future than to automatically come to the same conclusion as about four million other people who have just witnessed the event on TV.

In between cakes, the BBC radio cricket commentary team are renowned for their wonderfully irreverent descriptions of play (though I am some-times frustrated that their most interesting comments from a betting angle tend to come too late to be of any use). After an hour of the mornings play when four wickets have fallen for 20 runs it is not unu-sual to hear that one of them had inspected the pitch at 10 am and come to the conclusion that it was so poor that the batsmen would need a miracle to survive more than a couple of overs. Unfortunately they didnít tell us at the time, otherwise some of us would be showing quite a turn of pace to get to the phone and sell total runs.

This highlights a general principle whereby commentators seem loathed to reveal anything negative they are aware of, whether it be the state of a cricket pitch or the chances of the favourite in a Grand Prix.

Statements that anything is amiss with a favourite in any sporting contest can usually be taken as an indication that there is something seriously wrong. If the Channel 4 racing team donít like the look of the odds on favourite a couple of minutes before a race they might only be persuaded to hint that it is ëa little off colour compared with Newmarket 10 days agoí. The message behind this is that it will be lucky to be able to make its way to the start.

The sacred ëpitch reportí for televised cricket, generally considered a valuable guide to the run making potential of a wicket is unlikely to tell you the pitch is a total stinker. If the presenter refers to a ëfew small cracks that might open upí and hints that the surface is ëslightly unevení this is a fair indication that batsmen will find the bounce and movement so unpredictable that theyíll be lucky to get bat to ball whatsoever.

At the most basic level you need information on the markets themselves. This almost exclusively comes from Channel 4 Teletext and Skytext. One tends to find that, as a regular punter with the spread companies, a good proportion of your time is spent fretting as you wait for the sub-pages of the company to come round to the one you want. When the football season markets are displayed this can be a particularly gruelling test of patience as the number of sub-pages can be more than 12.

At present there is only one sporting daily paper in the UK, the tabloid format *Racing Post*. The demise of the *Sporting Life* in May 1998 is a substantial blow to those who crave facts in relation to Spread Betting, though the depth of information published by *The Racing Post* should be sufficient to keep spread enthusiasts busy over their breakfasts. At the time of writing the *Sporting Life* lives on in the form of an excellent website (*www.sporting-life.com*).

The Racing Post and the *Sporting Life* website are the main source of Spread Betting tips. This is a slightly problematical area as they necessarily have to keep up a constant supply of recommended bets and so do not have the luxury afforded to the rest of us of being selective. The difficulty in attempting to follow the papers selections is that inevitably a lot of other people, including the Spread Betting traders, are reading exactly the same comments. By the time you get on the phone the value element of the proposed bet will have disappeared as 100ís may be trying the same thing.

Where bets are based on solid new information rather than just a columnists opinion you can be pretty certain that attempts to get on at the stated price will almost certainly end in disappointment. Any information available on the news-stands at 6.30am can easily be assimilated by the spread companies who simply quote a new price to the first enquirer of the day at 9.30am. An example of this is when a ëcard happyí referee is named as official for a high profile game. This happened in the case of the crucial 1997 World Cup qualifier between Italy and England. The fact was prominently reported in the *Sporting Life* who highlighted that the quote ëcurrently availableí, i.e. yesterdayís, was far too low. In the circumstances it would have been pretty fruitless to try and get on at the previous dayís price that morning. As it turned out the referee obliged with a flurry of cards meaning that you could have bought the booking index at any point and still made a considerable profit in this case.

I am a big fan of the *Racing and Football Outlook*, published weekly on Tuesday. Although its coverage of Spread Betting per-se is not great, its football pages are amongst the most valuable and its lists of football odds for the following weekends games are the first in print. The fact that it is printed comparatively far in advance means many of its recommendations have to be made before any indications of odds are available (particularly racing tips).This might appear to make them less valid but in fact, if anything, demonstrates that some real thought has gone into selections rather than simply being swayed into agreeing with the odds on offer (which I suspect lets a lot of other correspondents down). Its sports tips always seem to be based on clear logic and it is particularly strong on golf with its contributions from Angus Loughran.

For those on-line the Internet offers a host of sites of some relevance though the task of picking out the quality from the rubbish can be arduous. The *Sporting Life/Press Association* site at *www.sporting-life.com* is the undisputed king with a depth of coverage that is frankly breathtaking. It maintains Spread Betting news sections for all the major sports with details of current prices and a database of statistics (particularly useful for racing) that can be delved into with ease. The whole service is free, which is particularly amazing since it isnít festooned with advertising.

The Racing Post website at *www.racing-post.com* offers an online version of the newspaper and specialises in a subscription-only horse racing form/information service - undoubtedly superb for enthusiasts of traditional gambling on racing but of somewhat less interest to spread bettors. There are a number of excellent directories of football/gambling sites and a number of search engines specifically for football related sites. This is particularly useful in searching out information on foreign teams. I found little difficulty in tracing a mass of information on Norwegian club, Tromso prior to their Cup Winners Cup tie with Chelsea. In fact there is more information on just about every soccer league in the World than one could ever want or need. Internet gambling newsgroups are generally full of useless advertising but a comparatively spam free and intelligent source of excellent racing/betting discussion can be found in *uk.sport.horseracing* - there is also some discussion of Spread Betting.

The Internet is primarily a goldmine of factual information. The work that must go into maintaining some of the larger sites must be huge considering few of them make money for those that put in so much time and effort. It took me only a short time to track down all the results from the World Cup first round stages since 1974 and indeed there exists a mammoth site which has a complete log of all football internationals (including friendly matches).

There are a vast number of sporting information books on the market, though the types of information they provide can frequently only be of limited interest to us. Sources such as the *Rothman's Football Yearbook* is useful in some respects; for example, I used a few back copies to ascertain whether the early rounds of the League Cup tended to produce more goals on average than league games. However the vast majority of the endless tables do not in any way shed light on spread markets we are likely to come across.

Any books that relate performances to odds offered at the time are, however, a major help. In this respect Keith Elliotís *The Golf Form book* is invaluable as it contains comprehensive details of betting markets and enables us to analyse, for example, the likely finishing positions of favourites. Other than on the purely informational side, books can play a useful part in determining betting strategy. Although somewhat out of date *The Punters Revenge* by Drapkin and Forsyth is one of only a handful of books to take analysis seriously. More recently Nick Mordinís *Betting for a Living* gives a pretty good idea of the depth of thought that has to go into racing to make it pay.

I have a genuine enthusiasm for anything published on sports gambling even if it is hopelessly wide of the mark. I have a collection of published systems which vary from the criminally exploitative to some that seem quite credible. They all have their uses in demonstrating how people think about their gambling and often get me wondering about aspects of markets I hadnít previously considered.

One can also see ëinformationí in terms of finding out what other people are thinking, and if you sense a weight of ill-informed opinion going in one particular direction, quietly take out a spread position going the opposite way. Looking at some of the contributions to Internet ëchatí forums, particularly relating to football, one gets a strong sense of what people are really thinking about sport and their reactions to results/ press coverage.

After Spread Betting for a while, it becomes clear that the influence of the weather on sporting results is extraordinary. If you were sure that you precisely knew what the weather would be doing during a sporting event at a particular location I would dare say that you could happily make a substantial income from Spread Betting. In its most basic form the weather can frequently determine if an event actually goes ahead. Cricket is particularly susceptible to this. As a consistent seller of runs I sometimes find myself jumping for joy at the sight of players coming off the field for a rain interruption. The prospect of rain in a golf tournament can radically effect the chances of individual players; some Grand Prix drivers are better suited to wet conditions; favourites in horseracing do worse in bad weather conditions; winning distances go up. The list is almost endless.

Currently, I am living quite close to Old Trafford Cricket ground which gives me a slight advantage over traders when it comes to test matches played in Manchester. In the hours leading up to a Test match, they are mostly gazing out of a window in Central London, whereas I can be fairly sure if there is a significant chance of rain and the possibility of a tricky wicket. If you happen to live near a racecourse staging a meeting and the heavens open shortly before any pictures are transmitted by SIS then you could similarly be at an advantage.

Everyone has their views on the reliability of UK weather forecasts. The only possible useful observation that I can make is that regional forecasts following local news programmes invariably exaggerate weather extremes. So if the forecast for Leeds in the national weather bulletin states that temperatures will average at around freezing you can usually be sure that this will have been spiced up to read -6°C (with the possibility of major disruption) for your local forecast.

When it comes to events in other countries a bit of weather information can go a long way. Here again the Internet can prove invaluable. It ís 7am the morning of the start of the U.S. Greensboro Open and you want to back a golfer who tends to give his best in sunny conditions. Will your man find the weather to his liking? Simply log on to the Yahoo weather page, type in ëGreensboroí and youíll get a complete five day forecast. If youíre still unsure someone from the Chemistry department of the University has probably got a web camera stuck out of a fourth floor window in which case you can see for yourself.

10 Good Times... and Bad

*I had given the day up as a bad deal when I was fatally
drawn to the markets on the final of the Eurovision
Song Contest held later that evening*

In any given week a spread account holder may have access to a vast range of markets and prices. Add to these the range of traditional betting opportunities covering an ever-increasing range of sports/events and the choice becomes bewildering. If just a single market is priced up incorrectly an astute individual is in a position to profit handsomely. The odds compilers and spread traders cannot afford to get it wrong. Hills and Ladbrokes, the two big names of UK bookmaking were taken to the brink of bankruptcy in the mid 1960ís by pricing errors on their football fixed odds coupons. British gambling history is littered with excellent coups, pricing errors and even one or two ësystemí based gambles that have netted their exponents huge sums. The heavily geared nature of Spread Betting means that any current-day pricing errors can be punished more severely by those quick enough to exploit them.

On reading accounts of past successes of others, one cannot help feeling a twinge of jealously towards those who pulled off these big gambles. Could there possibly be room in the highly competitive, professional and hi-tech world that is modern bookmaking for such opportunities to ever happen again? **Many readers will know the sensation of apparently having found some form of glorious loophole, 'system' or other form of heaven sent betting opportunity**, only for it to be shot down in flames on further analysis, or more critically, immediately having placed the momentous wager.

Good times...

In such a frame of mind I was looking forward to the General Election of 1997. The Labour Party had been out of power since 1979 but had been consistently more than 10 percentage points ahead in the opinion polls in the year prior to the election and were realistically looking at forming the next government. My interest in politics and electoral statistics had grown steadily for a number of years and I was keen to see the variety of odds that would be on offer. Though, in the early part of the year I did not suspect that the election would give rise to perhaps the greatest betting opportunity of my life.

At face value the election seemingly had little betting potential. Labour were 1/5 to win an overall majority, requiring a 5.5% swing from the Conservatives. However, there was the shadow of the fact that in the last election of 1992 the opinion polls were sufficiently wrong (overestimating the Labour support by 3% and underestimating conservative support by a similar percentage) to have predicted entirely the wrong result. This celebrated foul-up was uppermost in the minds of both the public and political commentators leading to a generalised reluctance throughout the country to believe a word the pollsters uttered. I tried arguing in vain with those who put forward the view that the polls could be not be trusted, reasoning that even if the same margin of error were to be repeated Labour would still win comfortably as they were averaging a lead of 16% in the polls.

Slowly something of a bandwagon effect started taking place. It seemed that everyone you spoke to felt it was going to be a close run event and individuals, whose opinions I tended to value, spoke confidently of the possibility of a shock Conservative win. This was echoed in much of the press, most notably of all the left wing *New Statesman*, which despite evidence to the contrary seemed excessively gloomy for the chances of a Labour success. The Labour Party itself attempted to play down their hopes of achieving a crushing victory leading Tony Blair himself to declare that, ìthis is not a Landslide countryî.

At this point I started taking a real interest in the betting opportunities and looking closely at the various chances of different types of results occurring. I had no complaints with the overall odds of 1/5 for an outright Labour majority but was interested in betting on the size of the overall majority. I armed myself with a copy of ëThe Voters Guide the General Electionî, an invaluable book for political ëtrainspottersí detailing the swings required by the main parties to win any of the 658 parliamentary constituencies.

The opinion polls were relatively static, though the Conservative sup- porting press highlighted any improvement in the Tories position and ignored any sign of slipping back. This gave the impression that the Conservatives were gaining consistently as these ëpositiveí polls were the only ones reported.

This ëtalking upí of Conservative fortunes aided anyone wishing to take out a gambling position against the Tories as even the most cur- sory comparison of the figures demonstrated that the Tory share of the vote was dead in the water. Taking the lower of the opinion poll esti- mates Labour appeared to be on course for 44% of the popular vote with the Conservatives trailing at 30%. In virtually no opinion polls were they registering above 30% at any time. I made allowance in my calculation for the fact that there may be a structural error in the polls of a similar nature to that of 1992, meaning Labour may only win 41% of the vote.

There was however a more tricky factor to consider. When converting the popular vote figures into the estimates of overall majorities there must be a standard formula. Some of these extrapolations were pub- lished - so that at a glance you could tell that Labourís majority would be in the region of, for instance, 60 seats if they had 42% to the Tories 34%. These standard formulas were likely to be inaccurate, however, because of the modern day phenomena of tactical voting, whereby vot- ers who wanted to oust the incumbent Tory MP would vote for the opposition party that were perceived to be in the best position to defeat the sitting MP in their particular constituency. The effect of this could be to ëconcentrateí Labours votes in the areas that they needed them most (to defeat Conservative MPs rather than pile up ëneedlessí votes in safe Labour seats.) If such tactical voting was reasonably widespread, as seemed might be the case, the popular vote/seats won calculations would need to be altered in favour of the Labour Party and the Liberal Democrats.

I had noticed that there were huge differences in these calculations between newspapers. Two papers would report the same poll result and come to alarmingly different conclusions as to what this would mean for the overall majority figure. I decided that a reasonably simple means of building the tactical voting factor in would be simply to add back the couple of percentage points that I had taken off Labourís popular-vote percentage in the first place in counter-acting the possible error in the opinion poll findings.

At this stage, about 10 days from the election itself, I had a fairly fixed impression that the final voting figure would be Labour 45% - Conservatives 30%. If any of the political pundits seemed to be talking sense about their interpretations of the opinion polls then I tended to place heavy emphasis in their predictions. David Butler, writing in the *Financial Times* has written a statistical analysis on many of the post-war elections and was consistently adamant that Labour were heading for a huge ëlandslideí majority. Whilst so many pundits were desperately trying to whip up some enthusiasm for a Tory recovery I tried to concentrate on his columns as I nervously considered how much I was going to wager.

Having laboriously gone through my ëVoters guideí, I managed to estimate which seats would be won by each party on the voting figures I had envisaged. I came to a final tally that had the Labour party winning by 163 seats. My method of converting the popular vote figures into an overall majority tally appeared to be in line with the method used by the *Daily Telegraph* which proved handy as they were printing the estimated overall majority virtually every day in large figures on the front page. With a week to go until polling it was hovering between 160 and 180.

I decided to leave a spread bet until after the final weekend of campaigning, and I turned my attentions to the odds on offer with the fixed odds companies for individual seats. On walking into a branch of William Hills in Stockport I found myself staring at the screens in disbelief at some of the prices offered on Labour candidates to win their individual seats. Initially catching my eye was a quote of 6/4 for the Labour candidate Anthony Coleman in Putney who required a 7.8% swing from the Conservatives to take the seat. Since I was estimating a 12% swing to Labour across the board this seemed exceedingly generous, especially as the Referendum Party leader was standing against Conservative David Mellor and could be expected to take a significant handful of votes from the Tories. Having placed a couple of small bets I discovered that Ladbrokes were offering a full range of odds on local candidates but these were only available in the individual constituencies themselves.

London had a concentration of seats where Labour needed swings of between five and 12%, the sort of range that was realistically within their reach. To take advantage of these prices the best course of action was to get to the Capital, arm myself with a tube travel card and start conducting my own campaign tour of the constituencies. Ladbrokes are generally renowned for being the most difficult bookmaker to beat. They always seem to be a step ahead of their rivals and when good betting opportunities exist it is almost never with Ladbrokes.

On this occasion, however, someone had been pushing the wrong buttons as the prices on a number of Labour candidates were astronomical. I was offered 2/1 for the Labour candidate in Putney, so long a price that I considered the possibility that they had incorrectly given me the price on another candidate and it would go down as a palpable error.

The following example illustrates my reasoning more clearly; I found a price of 5/4 for the Labour candidate, Martin Linton, in Battersea. He needed only a 4.6% swing from the Tories to win the seat. Nationally Labour needed 5.5% to win an overall majority. This was priced at 1/4. Therefore it made sense to me that the correct price for Battersea should have been in the region of 1/4 as well, if not lowerÖ

Even though Christmas had come very early for meat Ladbrokes, my personal favourite was Hills price of 11/4 for Paul Truswell, Labour candidate in Pudsey, West Yorkshire, requiring a very attainable 7.3% swing. I would honestly have priced up his chances at around 4/6. As I didnít take a trip to Pudsey I never discovered Ladbrokeís price for him, but had it been higher than Hills, which was the general pattern, I would possibly have rated it as the greatest wager of the decade.

I finally pitched in with the spread bet having read the Sundayís *Observer* report headed ëCabinet cull in prospect if voters take tactical routeí. This presented individual constituency polls which, as it turned out, fairly accurately reflected the events of polling day itself. From the report it looked conceivable that Labour might achieve a majority of pushing 200.

On Monday I assumed that the *Observer* had laid to rest any thoughts that there was going to be anything other than a catastrophic defeat for the Tories. I imagined this would have an enormous effect on the spreads which had, up to this point, been hovering around the Labour majority of 90 mark. This strangely didnít seem to be the case so I pitched in with a number of trades buying at prices between 94 and 100, and followed this with another round of individual constituency bets placed in small denominations in a number of outlets plus a few fixed odds bets covering the range of majority of figures that I predicted. Ladbrokes kindly offered 14/1 for a majority of 141-160, 16/1 for 161-180 and 20/1 for 181-200. It was subsequently stated in a BBC documentary that the weekendís poll figures finished any lingering hopes in Conservative Central Office and that Prime Minister, John Major, was resigned to a massive defeat during the final few days of the campaign.

At the last moment, on the afternoon of voting, I was still scurrying around trying to get on more overall majority bets, when, at about 4pm, the major firms finally closed the election books. By this time I had amassed liabilities large enough to sink me without trace had it all gone wrong. There followed a few nervous hours before the first results at 11pm. When the BBC ëexití poll was published at 10pm it predicted a Labour landslide and though the swings to Labour were moderate in the first few seats declared, gradually swings of 11% and more began to be reported. In fact the spreads shot up unjustifiably high and I decided to sell Labourís majority back at 194 - the eventual majority was 179 (also enabling me to collect on one of the fixed odds overall majority bets). By 10am the next morning the individual constituency bets had all gone in my favour with one constituency to come, where I was to experience the one setback of the ëcampaigní, when Brecon and Radnor was captured by the Lib Dems.

All in the all, it was the most profitable day of my betting life with a profit of nearly £5,500. It was not exactly a great feat of skill and I certainly didnít have access to any information that anyone else couldnít have gained from spending half an hour in their local library.

...And the bad

Having recounted my moment of glory it would only be fair to reflect on what I rate as my worst bet of all time. **Inevitably I could take my pick from a fair number of bets that I came to regret almost immediately**, but one stands out as having a particularly duff quality to it.

Although the financial loss was tiny (I have yet to experience any degree of Spread Betting ëmeltdowní, though I dare say I will go through the experience someday) - this particular spread wager was dreadful because of a fundamental error in assessing the market.

Saturday the 9th May 1998 must rank as the poorest Saturday for sport as far back as I remember. Most account holders will know that days come along where, in the absence of anything more purposeful, a spread bet is just about compulsory to give the day a bit of a fizz. When such feelings coincide with rotten sport warning bells should start ringing. The climax to the Premier League was scheduled for the next day, the racing was seemed mostly sub-Class E and the BBC had hours of solid coverage of the Badminton horse trials (as yet not the subject of much Spread Betting interest).

I had given the day up as a bad deal when I was fatally drawn to the markets on the final of the Eurovision Song Contest held later that evening. I began to concoct an elaborate theory concerning the result. In the absence of anything remotely worth a gamble throughout the rest of the day, and the fact that the Eurovision Song Contest draws a massive TV audience in the UK, I began to convince myself that there might be a lot of ësillyí money floating around with account holders just itching to get on the musical....eh....extravaganza.

Since there was only one market generally available, that on the number of points the UK entry would score, I figured that it might be subject to some fairly heavy trading. Knowing that British competitors in international sport tended to be bought up by patriotic money as the event time approaches I decided to wait until the last moment and then sell. The sell point of the market in the morning stood at 112 points. If I waited long enough I was sure that I might get 120, at which point Iíd go in. Whatever the competition I tend to let my wallet rule my patriotic spirit and therefore am always looking to sell British competitors performance, whatever their field of activity.

In this case I could see no reason to change the strategy. With a lunatic German entry and the transsexual ëDana Internationalí representing Israel I couldnít foresee the UK being in the top two. Also, for the first time, members of the public were to decide the result in the competing nations. This, I decided, would lead to the spread of the points being ëflattenedí (less difference than usual between the points for the winner and the points for those low in the poll) as voting would be even more along regional lines. Having got this far I set about an estimation of UK points for which I eventually decided on a figure of around 98, putting them in the region of fourth place.

As I predicted the quote steadily moved up and, as the entries were being presented, the quote point hit my target of 120, prompting me to sell. For some bets, as soon as the event itself starts, you know youíre on to a good thing. On this occasion I didnít even get as far as the results of the first countries votes before I realised I had made a fairly critical error. As the announcer went through the voting procedure explaining that juries would award scores of 1, 2, 3, 4, 5, 6, 7, 8, 10 and 12 points I could foresee defeat instantly - I had calculated the UK score on the basis of juries awarding 2, 4, 6, 8, 10 and 12 points. In effect this meant that there were vastly more points to be allocated than I had anticipated.

As the evening wore on it was clear that Iíd be punished for this incredibly dim mistake. The UK didnít win, but did amass 169 points. I got what I deserved.

The obvious lesson here is to make absolutely sure one knows precisely how a market works and how an event is scored. There are plenty of pitfalls. Are you sure that, in confidently selling football shirt numbers, the teams are not going to appear wearing squad numbers, some of them in the 30ís? Are you absolutely convinced that the tennis match in which you sold supremacy is over three sets and not five? **I would guess a sizeable proportion of spread bets are placed by people who have missed a vital piece of information, that if they were aware of, would have put them off placing the trade.** Having confessed to getting in this position myself I am determined that, for me, history will not repeat itself.

11 Market Focus: Golf

Of all betting sports, golf genuinely offers those with in-depth knowledge of form a real opportunity to beat the spreads

The golf betting fraternity in the UK could best be described as small but serious. For them, and anyone tempted to have a golf bet, the emergence of Spread Betting could not have come too soon. Fixed odds golf punters have had to tolerate the highest bookmakerís margins throughout all betting markets. The favourite in a golf tournament will usually be offered at around 10/1. Once you get out to 10th favourite the odds rise to more than 25/1. At first glance these may look quite palatable, however adding up the associated percentages of all the odds on offer reveals a depressing truth. In a field of 150 competitors (a fairly standard field for major competitions) the total percentage will add up to near the 150% mark. To overcome such a large margin consistently to make a long term profit is virtually impossible. To make matters worse, margins on so called match bets (where one player is paired with another - the lowest score over 72 holes wins) are being increased by the major firms.

The coverage of golf by the spread firms is exhaustive. The US and European tours are covered extensively so a week should not go by without the opportunity to bet on a tournament. The situation is improved further by the widespread coverage of golf on Sky TV. Golf is a ënaturalí sport for Spread Betting as the game itself is determined by the number of shots it takes to get the ball in the hole and this figure has a high variability, unlike goals in soccer which has a low variability. It is debatable, however, whether golf will win new fans through Spread Betting as so much of the vital action takes place away from the gaze of the TV camera. If youíve got a bet on a player to finish lower than second place and they do not figure on the main leader board, then a few hours watching the coverage is unlikely to reveal much about his progress, let alone show much of the action that is relevant to his finishing position.

Of all betting sports, golf genuinely offers those with in depth knowledge of form a real opportunity to beat the spreads. Only the form of the top 20 or so players in the world is publicly discussed and with such large fields and an enormous number of tournaments, those who properly analyse the factors that contribute to good/bad performances can expect to be one step ahead. **The form book in golf is fiendishly difficult to assess correctly and the variability of results is quite astounding.** A player winning a tournament and proceeding to miss the cut in his next contest is the difference between first and 90th place, possibly in the space of a week. In no other betting sport is their such volatility of performances. This is rather like Manchester United finishing first in the Premiership one season and (if it were possible) third from bottom in the third division in the next season.

The staple golf spread bet offered on all tournaments by all the companies is that of *Winning Positions*:

Tiger Woods	15 - 17
Davis Love	16 - 18
Colin Montgomerie	20 - 22

Here the winner makes up at one so we have a very rare occurrence in spread markets; in this instance you would sell if you thought the golfer was going to do well (achieve a better position than his spread) and buy to do badly (achieve a worse position than his spread). It is worth bearing in mind that a number of players may tie for each position. If the three players named in the example tied in second place they would each make up at three (the sum of the positions they ëtake upí; two, three and four, divided by the number of players tied). The maximum make-up is generally 50 which may only account for the top third of all the competitors. Therefore a buyer is not well rewarded if the player backed against does particularly badly, for instance if he misses the cut by a long way.

Intuitively when offered a *Winning Positions* spread of 15 - 17 one would be tempted to sell. For a favourite to finish in the top 15 positions does not seem a tall order. In fact a look at the fate of favourites in golf tournaments soon tempers this view. The stark facts are that only

10 - 15% of competitors who figure in the top four of the betting market actually go on to finish in a top four position. This means that the majority of golf tournaments final placings contain none of those in the top four of the betting. The major implication of this is that one should not be drawn into the betting market and imagine that the result will mirror, even in the most tenuous way, the shape of the betting. Do not be surprised if the favourites finish 28th, 35th, missed cut, missed cut. The pre-tournament focus on the perceived advantages of the favourites should similarly be given comparatively little weight.

The key to finding bets on the winning positions market is, on the positive side, to pick out a player whose recent form is consistent, though it need not necessarily be consistently ëgoodí. A player whose last three finishes were 18th, 19th and second, and without a tournament top four finish in their career is possibly a better bet than one with a record of first, missed cut, and 40th whose recent win will be generally recognised by the betting public. On the negative side a high profile but volatile player in terms of winning positions makes the best ëbuyí (i.e. to do badly).

Super Seven indices have become a standard market on golf. Here just seven listed player count on a 50 : 25 : 10 index. Since no other players count, the ëwinnerí, who is assigned 50 points may, in terms of the tournament, finish well out of contention. My discussion of *Super Seven's* as relating to football holds here. The volatility and unpredictability of golf means that buying any form of supremacy of one player over another is a dangerous tactic. The seven chosen for the index are invariably the favourites who may start between 8/1 and 16/1 in the outright fixed odds betting. The difference between 8/1 and 16/1 looks quite large at first sight and yet if you convert the odds into their associated percentages, (8/1 = 11.1%: 16/1 = 5.88 %) the gap between an 11% chance and a 6% chance looks less wide.

In terms of the realistic chances of players at these odds winning, having taken out the bookmakers margin, the figures are more like 7.7% and 4.1% respectively. On a *Super Seven* index it is worth looking at the relative differences between players quoted. As an example, imagine Colin Montgomerie is quoted at 15 - 18 on the spread. Taking the mid point (16.5) we can calculate the percentage this represents of all the points on offer; 50 + 25 + 10 = 85 points on offer;

$$\frac{100}{85} = 1.17$$

$$1.17 \times 16.5 \text{ (midpoint)} = 19.30\%$$

On this occasion Montgomerieís spread represents one fifth of the total points on offer. If all the players were of equal ability you would expect them all to be given spreads whose midpoint was one seventh of the total points on offer. This would equate to spreads of 10.5 - 13.5.(a midpoint of 12) It is easy to look at Montgomerieís quote of 15 - 18 and be enticed with the vast profit promised of 32 points for a win and even a two point profit for coming second, especially as the down side seems reasonably small. However I would prefer to see a buy at 18 in terms of it being six points worse than the ëcorrectí expected make-up of 12 if all the players had an equal chance. I would be far more inclined to look at players whose quotes fell below this ëchanceí thresholdí of 12. On many tournaments you will find more than one *Super Seven* Index being offered, perhaps one on the top American Players and another on top Europeans.

Head-to-head match betting gives an opportunity to back one player against another even if it is a stroke play event where the players are not directly competing against each other. These forms of ëmatchí bets are common across a range of sports and tend to be designed so players of more or less equal ability are paired. So a quote of Forsbrand / Parvenik 0.5 - 1.5 over a 72 hole tournament means that if Forsbrand finishes with 284 compared to Parvenikís 287 he has achieved a supremacy of three (287 - 284). Sellers at 0.5 will incur a loss of 2.5 points whereas buyers at 1.5 will achieve a profit of 1.5.

Since the pairings for match bets tend to be very close in the betting I am generally put off from having to concede any head start in a match bet, and in golf this particularly holds true. You have to be mighty confident in the ëfavouriteí to buy their supremacy rating. Where there can be such a huge variation in performances from tournament to tournament I always feel more comfortable ignoring any match bet buys and automatically look for supremacy sells.

Spread markets tends to concentrate on those that head the betting, meaning that the usual skill of finding good value bets from the less fancied in the field is generally difficult to apply. Nevertheless there are new markets provided by the spread firms which open up a range of betting opportunities. One of the specialised markets which I follow closely is that on the number of players breaking par in the course of a tournament.

Of all the spread markets available this is perhaps the one most dependent on the weather conditions. Good conditions with little wind contribute to a high make-up; rain, poor visibility and, most importantly, high winds are almost certain to mean a low make-up. Anyone a step ahead of the spread companies with their meteorological predictions is really at an advantage. Even during the course of a days play the difference between those players going out in good weather compared to starters who have to endure poor conditions is highly significant and a little knowledge here can go a long way.

The difficulty of the course is, not surprisingly, a major factor in determining both the number of players who break par and the final score of the winner (which can be backed separately). Of relevance here is that I have never heard of a case of a course greenkeeper stating that their 18 holes are playing incredibly easy and the players will blitz it with record scores. On the contrary the ëinformationí that appears generally is that the rough is long, the fairways impossibly narrow and pin placements testing.

This is really the opposite of what happens in cricket where pitches that are pronounced good for batting turn out anything but. In my experience these so called ëtoughí courses are only made genuinely tough if there is rotten weather about, otherwise the abilities of modern players seem to be capable of tackling even the stiffest of tests when it comes to course preparation. When I come across this sort of situation I immediately start looking to sell the winning score and buy the number of players that will break par. The trick is to try and trade when the story has been fully assimilated and those anxious to cash in on the prophecies of doom have moved the markets.

I have heard it said that an individualís true temperament comes out on a golf course. Certainly I am aware that the emotional ups and downs of golf are probably only comparable to those experienced in Spread Betting! The degree to which golf is a game of the mind as well as technique is probably the main contributory factor to the variability of tournament results. From a betting point, as in all sports, it is vital to be able to draw upon information which is not available/taken into account by others. It is possible to delve into the minutiae of golf form, if one so wishes, to pick out factors that give a particular competitor the edge in any given tournament.

An overriding factor seems to be the performance of a player when last at the course, or even the country, of the tournament. In fact, a good record on a particular course is probably a more significant factor than current form. The type of course ranks as factor number two - essentially unchallenging but very long course favour those with long driving capabilities; shorter, narrow courses benefit those with accuracy, not length off the tee. Be aware though, that in punditís eyes, virtually all golfers seem to be equally brilliant at all aspects of their game. They are not about to inform you of a playerís erratic short iron play and laughable bunker shots. This ëhorses for coursesí approach requires considerable ability to sift through large amounts of golf form information, but ultimately is the means by which the small fraternity of golf betting enthusiasts look to get ahead.

Possibly the most complex consideration is the variation between players ability to perform well in poor weather. To back a player such as Phil Mickelson, who is considered to cope well in bad conditions, on a day when a gale is actually blowing requires both an in depth knowledge of the game and access to a decent weather forecast.

I am not totally convinced by the argument that players find it unusually hard to win consecutive tournaments because they are unable to withstand the high levels of concentration required. I tend to think that the simple explanation is that in fields where 100 competitors stand a realistic chance of winning the likelihood of any single player winning two in a row is rather remote, irrespective of their prior performance.

The Tiger Woods ëphenomenaí, as it tends to be dubbed. is certainly one of the more incredible sporting stories of the decade and also one of the most intriguing in terms of betting. Woods took golf off the back pages of the papers and into the headlines by being the youngest player to win the US Masters. The style in which this victory was achieved, aided by an average drive distance of 323 yards suggested that the professional game was about to be totally dominated by one man in a way in which was unprecedented.

In the wake of his victory everyone seemed to want to back him at any price forcing his fixed odds win price down to an amazing 9/2 for a tournament. Though there were obviously punters trying to get on in droves it was not easy to tell whether he was genuinely a popular champion who was overvalued in the betting or the subject of what might be best described as patronising and generally somewhat negative press coverage that played down his true potential.

I wrestled with this problem in the run up to the British Open in 1997 having read all manner of exceptionally snooty articles to the effect that he was very talented, but for him to come and win the British Open at the first attempt was simply ënot on, old boyí. In the end I came down on the side of the Woodís fan club, as it proved, a wrong decision as he was decisively beaten in his spread match with Colin Montgomerie that I had targeted. Nevertheless if he continues to create as much interest in the game as he has done so far he will contribute many more headaches for golf punters trying to assess the level of his greatness.

12 Financial Markets

The stock market frequently behaves in a
seemingly paradoxical way

S peculation on the financial markets is regarded as the respectable, institutional face of gambling. The fundamentals of Spread Betting are based on techniques developed from financial markets and presently two companies, IG Index and City Index, run financial trading services in parallel with their sports betting. The ëIGí in IG Index stands for ëInternational Goldí, a reference to their origins in 1974 as a company trading derivatives on the price of gold. City Index have offered financial Spread Betting since their inception in 1983.

For private individuals wishing to play the financial markets these two spread companies offer an invaluable service. Otherwise, participation in financial markets requires enlisting the services of a broker, who can be frequently less than keen to service clients taking out relatively small positions. Brokerage fees are payable, which in themselves can substantially eat away at any profits. In addition, dealing profits may be taxable. Whereas private individual share ownership has broadened considerably in the last 20 years, active participation in the financial markets has remained a largely professional activity.

The two spread companies offering financial trading do not promote their services with quite the same aggressive intent as their sports betting operations. Indeed the stipulations regarding the opening of financial accounts are somewhat more stringent than those governing sports betting accounts. Aside from being able to provide proof of £5,000 of liquid funds, IG clients are asked to provide evidence of ërelevant experience of dealing in financial marketsí. Derivative speculation on the stock market can entail enormous risks and the spread companies must, by law, ensure that clients are able to meet their debts should the worst happen. The financial crash in October 1987, dubbed ëBlack Mondayí, left a handful of Spread Betting clients with liabilities of over half a million pounds. There are serious consequences for the spread companies should even one debtor of such magnitude fail to clear their account.

Risk warnings aside, the minimum stakes accepted by the spread firms are considerably lower than those on the main trading markets themselves. City Index requires a minimum stake of £5 per point on the FTSE (£10 with IG Index). This compares with a £25 minimum for trading direct on the LIFFE market. The degree of risk can be contained by arranging a stop-loss mechanism guaranteeing that an individual trade is automatically closed should the market move against you to a specified level. In addition ëlimit ordersí may be placed whereby a bet is opened for you if the market reaches a pre-determined level.

The mechanics of betting on the financial markets are the same as those in sports betting. A spread of 5475 - 5485 might be quoted on the ëdailyí FTSE 100. If you thought the index was likely to rise during the day you might ëbuyí at 5485 for £100 per point. If the index closed at 5495 you would make 5495 minus 5485 (10 points) multiplied by your unit stake (£100), giving a profit of £1000. If the market closed at 5480 you lose the difference between your buy point of 5485 and the closing price of 5480 (5 points) multiplied by your unit stake (£100) leaving a loss of £500.

As with sports betting, positions can be traded in running or partially closed at any time during trading hours. In fact the trading hours of the spread markets are greater than those of the main UK stock markets themselves. Spread markets are generally operating between 7.30am and 9pm so bets can frequently be made when the underlying market has ceased trading. The 9pm close of trading hours corresponds with the close of the Dow Jones in the United States so any marked movements in the US can be traded-upon immediately rather than having to wait until the opening of the London market the following day (when there may be major fluctuations as a result of the American activity).

Financial Spread Markets

B oth City Index and IG index offer a range of markets, though very specialised knowledge is required to even contemplate trading the more esoteric indices. Of primary importance to UK account holders are the markets on the daily FTSE and the quarterly FTSE. The FTSE 100 became the main measure of the stock market since its use began in 1983. This index measures a sample of the performance of the top 100 companies in the UK and uses weighting mechanisms which mean that it tracks the performance of the 2500+ companies listed on the stock market as a whole.

The ëDaily FTSEí, as its name implies makes up at 16.10 every week-day. City Index quote a six point spread when the underlying market is open (between 0830 and 1610) and an eight point spread at other times that their trading desk is open (0730 - 0830 and 1630 - 2115). This is not a particularly attractive market for the first timer to financial betting as the size of the spread is high in proportion to the ënormalí fluctuations of the FTSE in a single day. For an individual trying to trade on ëbreakingí financial news the daily FTSE market may be the place to operate, but the fact that large stakes need to be employed in order to take advantage of small fluctuations in the market leaves this type of ëday traderí particularly susceptible to enormous financial losses should the market suddenly turn against them.

Of greater interest to those wishing to speculate on the FTSE is the quarterly market. At the time of writing City Index were offering the following quote:

Expiry date	Market	Spread	Previous Close	Current Price (17 Aug.)
18 Sept.	FTSE 100	5475 - 5485	5520	5455

The value of the FTSE on the previous dayís close was 5455; the price at closure of the previous quarter was 5520 (indicating that the market had experienced a fall in the previous two months). The spread is essentially the firmís prediction of the likely level of the FTSE on 18 Sept. City Index predict that the market will rise by 25 points in the period between the present date (17 Aug.) and the expiry date (18 Sept.). From the above information it is clear that the FTSE lost 65 points in the two months prior to 17 Aug, though the spread implies that it will recover to put on 25 points in the remaining month of the quarter.

If you feel that their estimate is too high then you might be tempted to sell at 5475. If you feel that the FTSE will outperform their spread you would be looking to buy at 5485. The spread will change constantly dependent upon market conditions at the time, so a sudden downward movement may cause the quarterly spread to readjust. Of course, as in sports betting there is no obligation to wait until the market makes-up on 18 Sept., one can take a profit or a loss at any time.

Information on the spread companies markets and prices is currently not as accessible to the public as their sports prices. City Index publish their most actively traded markets on Channel 4 text but otherwise prices for full range of markets are only available by contacting the companies direct or on the specialised news feeds such as Reuters and Bloomberg. The companiesí Internet sites have further details of financial markets. These include:

Stock Index Futures

FTSE 100 Index	Wall Street Index
Standard and Poors 500 Index	DAX 30 Index
IBEX 35	MIB 30
OMX (Stockholm)	Swiss Market
Hang Seng Index	Nikkei Dow

In addition IG Index allow futures on a selection of major UK individual stocks.

Currency Futures

Sterling to a number of major currencies (US Dollar; French Franc; Japanese Yen; Swiss Franc: German DM)
US Dollar to major currencies
German DM to major currencies

Government Bond Futures

UK, US, German, French, Italian, German, Spanish and Japanese government bonds

Interest Rate Futures

Sterling, Eurodollar, Euromark, Pilbor, Eurolira, Euroswiss, Euroecu (all 3 month expiry).

Commodities

Gold, Silver, Platinum, Copper, Cocoa, Coffee, Sugar, Corn, Orange Juice, Pork Bellies, Potatoes, Soyabeans, Wheat, Crude Oil, Gas Oil.

The worldís major currencies are traded to fractions of a unit. Markets generally make-up monthly. Hence a quote of £/$ 16120 - 16150 (9 Sept.) is inviting sellers who think that the US dollar rate will be lower than $1.6120 to every pound on 9 Sept., and buyers who predict that the number of dollars to the pound will exceed $1.6150. Small to medium sized businesses may use Spread Betting as a means of hedging against currency fluctuations that could effect the value of their imports/exports. It should be noted that the foreign exchange markets trade continuously as London, Wall Street and Tokyo are active at different times throughout the 24 hour clock. This is generally not the case in sports betting. A position on a foreign exchange market can mean the market can turn against you while you sleep.

To consider trading commodities futures one needs to be in touch with the market to a degree that puts these types of markets beyond the scope of most private individuals.

City Index offer a number of economic ëspecialí bets. A long running market has been offered on the number of countries that join European Monetary Union. The initial spread of 4.5 - 5.5 was steadily brought up as it became clear that UK media speculation that the whole project would end in failure was mostly a fantasy of the predominantly anti-European press.

Speculating on the FTSE 100

For a first timer to financial markets the quarterly market on the UK FTSE 100 index is likely to be most attractive. The index is discussed widely and information about the historical movements and likely future trends of the index is relatively easy to find in comparison to the more specialised markets on offer by the spread firms.

The occasional spectacular collapse of the FTSE 100 index and its predecessor the FT 30 index, is perhaps uppermost in the minds of the public, though in general terms the stock market has shown a steady upward trend in modern times. The exception to this was a significant slump in the 1970ís: in January 1969 the FTSE hit 521 and it took until January 1982 for the index to decisively break thorough this point again. The 1980ís showed unprecedented strengthening of the index and there has been another doubling of the value of the index through the 1990ís, outperforming all other forms of investment.

Although the stock market crash of October 1987 was catastrophic for many investors it was the pace of the crash rather than its overall scale which was fundamentally alarming. In fact the FTSE 100 ended the year 2% higher than its opening figure. The crash was intensified by computer programmes that automatically sold stock when a predetermined low price has been hit. In itself this triggered a wave of selling activity that could not have been so swift before the days of computerised trading technology.

For those holding actual stock, the loss in its value was comparatively short lived. But for anyone buying the quarterly FTSE the results would be devastating. There is no reason to suspect that such a crash could not occur again and this must be kept firmly in the mind of potential players of the FTSE market.

By trading on the quarterly FTSE one is taking a short to medium term view. Trading on such a basis is termed ëspeculationí. This is in contrast to the majority of ordinary stock market investors who hold stocks with a view to long term capital growth. The aim of the speculator is to take advantage of trends - for example, to identify when an upward turn will keep strengthening or conversely identify reasons why a sudden drop may be just around the corner. The FTSE 100 displays a generalised upward trend punctuated with a number of peak and troughs of various intensities. For the majority of the time the quarterly quote offered by the spread firms will be higher than the current market price. It is the quoted spread figure that must be used as the basis of ones analysis. Will the market reach the buy side of the quote or is a fall imminent which will give the potential to buy back at a profit?

FTSE Analysis

Some of the basic principles of sports betting apply to the financial markets. If everyone is using the same techniques of analysis then all your fellow traders are making the same decisions and the market will correspondingly move before a trade can be struck. If the wicket for a forthcoming test series looks dire and every newspaper has been discussing it then that information is already built into the price that is offered. The only way of trading on the information is if you think it is false or fundamentally over valued in its effect on the market. With the cricketing analogy, you may consider trading against the expectation that the wicket is bad, for instance by buying the number of runs predicted in the whole series.

Similar forces are at work with stock market ëtipsí. The Sunday papers recommend stocks that the readers should buy. Incidentally, financial editors of different papers mysteriously tip the same shares rather too frequently, which suggests that their ëexclusiveíadvice may come from the same source (who, no doubt, is keen to bolster a particular share price). Come Monday morning the share prices of firms that are the subject of the tipsters recommendations put on a surge before anyone can phone their broker. It is not uncommon to witness the share price of tipped companies slide back to their baseline position a few weeks after they are tipped. The lesson here has to be the same as in sports betting - Information that everyone knows is not worth having.

This factor should be kept in mind when looking at the ëtechnical analysisí of the stock market. Technical analysis simply refers to the examination of mathematical trends in the movement of the index in order to gain information about the current trends. The foundation of this type of approach is that the markets are essentially led by group behaviour. If the market has risen consistently for a number of months technical analysts, or ëchartistsí as they are otherwise known, may look at the history of similar periods in an effort to predict how the market might respond.

This perception of how speculators react *en-masse* gives rise to the expressions ëbull marketí (where prices are rising and the ëbullsí buy shares expecting them to rise in value allowing them to sell back at a higher price in the near future), and ëbear marketí (where prices are falling and shares are sold in the expectation of buying back at a cheaper price).

Much beloved of chartists is the examination of moving averages or trend lines. When looking at a graph of the recent history of the FTSE 100 it may appear as a convoluted series of peaks and troughs with little discernible pattern. Calculating the moving average is the means by which a smooth trend line can be superimposed over the very short term fluctuations. The longer the period of time taken into consideration when performing the calculation, the smoother the line will be; if the trend line is too smooth it is not sensitive to pick up a change of direction in the market; conversely if the period of time is too short the trend line will appear too jagged and unclear to make the direction of the trend discernible. Plotting the 13 week moving average is deemed a suitable compromise. Here an average is taken of the previous 13 weekís closing figures. At the end of a week the new closing figure is included and the oldest figure drops out of the calculation so that only 13 weeks figures are ever used. For example:

Week Ending	Closing price	13 Week Moving Average
8 July (1)	5676	-
15 July (2)	5696	-
22 July (3)	5720	-
29 July (4)	5723	-
5 Aug. (5)	5761	-
12 Aug. (6)	5739	-
19 Aug. (7)	5788	-
26 Aug. (8)	5803	-
2 Sep. (9)	5789	-
9 Sep. (10)	5837	-
16 Sep. (11)	5821	-
23 Sep. (12)	5802	-
30 Sep. (13)	5845	5769
7 Oct. (14)	5848	5782
14 Oct. (15)	5890	5797
21 Oct. (16)	5910	5811
28 Oct. (17)	5862	5822
4 Nov. (18)	5872	5831

When plotted on a graph the actual weekly figures display considerable variation in a semi-random fashion, but the moving averages display the upward trend in an almost linear fashion. It is generally believed that a change in direction of the 13 week moving average almost certainly signals a fundamental change in the marketís direction that cannot be put down to a short term variation. If you had a quote on the quarterly FTSE for December it would be possible to continue this trend line and discover whether the quote is higher or lower. This gives an excellent indication of how the quote has been pitched in relation to the current trend.

ëDow theoryí is a specific branch of technical analysis that seeks to establish patterns in the fluctuations of stock market indices for predictive purposes. Three distinct cycles are said to dominate the structure of the index:

Primary movements

The generalised direction of the market where prices are seen to move in one direction for a long period (up to a 4 year trend).

Secondary reactions

Shorter term swings in the opposite direction to the primary trend. These characteristically last an average of 4 to 5 weeks and generally account for around half the previous primary movement.

Random daily movements

Inconsequential chance fluctuations which have no bearing on the overall trend.

The cyclic variations described in Dow Theory appear to be the result of speculators identifying and trading on a trend. When an upward trend is noted the improvement in share prices is reinforced by hordes of investors coming on-board. The downturn, which is characteristically sharper than the rise, comes when shares are suddenly perceived to be overvalued. The haste to exit the market is self-perpetuating, and only when demand dries up significantly do the bulls start off the whole cycle again by purchasing stock at low prices.

Dow theory originated at the turn of the century and remains a cornerstone of market analysis, though any technical analysis is bound to be something of an art form.

Assigning meaning to Stock Market movements

There is a school of thought which holds that the stock markets are essentially a chaotic system whose fluctuations are largely the result of random acts and little meaning can be assigned to the patterns which result. To reinforce this theory there is a range of evidence to suggest that professional analysts fare little better than amateurs who simply play the stock market by chance. If this is the case then it would indicate that no amount of ëknowledgeí will put the speculator at an advantage compared to his fellow players. For a full explanation of how chance and chaos affect the fluctuations of the stock markets readers may like to refer to A Mathematician Reads a Newspaper by J. A. Paulos which provides an excellent summary of how random events tend to be interpreted as meaningful.

Speculation in the British media as to the state of the economy and the stock market is a highly developed journalistic enterprise. One of the striking features of comment on stock market movements is the way in which hindsight provides the explanation of why a FTSE trend has been established.

Sports gamblers will know this syndrome. It is easy to say that Brazil lost the 1998 World Cup because of their star player Ronaldo having a ëfití the previous night leading to arguments over team selection the dressing room. What would the explanation been had Brazil won? The tension in the team sharpened their appetite for one last Herculean effort?

The stock market frequently behaves in a seemingly paradoxical way. One of the most marked surges in the FTSE in recent history took place from mid-January to the end of April 1991. This actually coincided with the Gulf War, one of the more potentially destructive events to threaten the major world economies, particularly as oil supplies were jeopardised. The reason given for this sudden jump was that a downward correction to the FTSE had already occurred in August of the previous year when Iraq had invaded Kuwait. The leap in share prices that took place shortly beginning of armed conflict was put down to ëinvestors realising that the war was going better than expectedí.

This phenomena, where a primary movement in stock price is deemed to already have taken place long before the pivotal even, is particularly evident in discussion of individual shares. It is common to hear on financial bulletins that ìit was announced that there was a fall in interim profits for Nuts and Bolts PLC by one million pounds; shares rose 12pî. Here it is reasoned that those with their ear to the ground had already pushed the share price down on the basis of information trickling out that company profits were forecast to be down. As this was well in advance of the official announcement it is assumed that the rise in share price is the market expressing its view that the news is not as bad as expected.

Even if one is able to isolate the main economic indicators that are liable to affect the stock market it may be impossible to judge whether they will positively or negatively impact on the price. The ëEfficient Market Hypothesisí (EMH) states that prices take into account all available information and therefore cannot be predicted to any degree better than chance alone.

The financial markets display one characteristic that is strikingly different from sports betting in that there is no final definitive ëeventí that decides the make -up. In the run up to the World Cup the movement in the spread markets is largely the result of reactions to news, differing perceptions as to the strength of the teams etc. This element of manoeuvring is all there is in the financial markets. There is no decisive conclusion where the ëcorrectí value of the FTSE is calculated in the same way in which two teams battle it out on a football field.

Newcomers will require a considerable degree of discipline for trading any financial market. Many trades remain open far longer than a sports trade and it is therefore vital to set parameters within which one must stick rigidly. In considering a sell trade on the FTSE at what point will a rise in the market demonstrate that your original trade is incorrect? You might decide that a rise of 40 points from the mid point is enough to persuade you that the loss should be taken and no further funds can be risked. Correspondingly a profit target should be set and when this is achieved the trade closed.

By their nature, financial markets are virtually open-ended and highly volatile. Though the minimum stakes are small in comparison to those required by the actual LIFFE market they are substantial when compared to the minimum stakes required by the spread firms for sports betting. Those considering trading financial markets must satisfy themselves that they are fully aware of the risks involved.

14 Spread Psychology

At every opportunity the emphasis should be on looking for 'negative' bets - i.e. precisely the types of wagers that other account holders do not seem generally comfortable with

Spread Betting is distinct from its traditional counterpart in the unforgiving exactitude of the results of the wager. In the comparatively safe world of traditional odds betting, where you know precisely what your potential losses are, there can only be two results: you either win, or you lose. Unless you are consistently backing odds-on shots the majority of bets will be losers. The hope must be that the winners are at big enough prices to compensate. A racing enthusiast betting on horses in the 4/1 region realistically knows that there is a slightly less than 20% chance that any single bet will be a winner. He is used to this sort of win ratio and so the disappointment of losing can only be mild as he has to bear it on the vast majority of occasions. If the horse doesnít win there is always the apparent consolation that it ran a good race, that the price represented value, or any other solace you care to think of.

The average punterís philosophy generally is ëthereís always the next dayí. **Losing can be a minor annoyance punctuated by a thrilling win.** Spread Betting is markedly different. You get a precise ëresultí on every bet, starkly written on your account statement. The amount you win or lose is a direct reflection of the result and, by implication, your skill at reading the event - there can be little room for interpreting the result in a favourable light.

Like most TV detectives the character of ëFitzí, the forensic psychologist in ITVís popular police drama *Cracker*, laboured under a major aberration of personality - an addiction to gambling on the horses. In one episode he gives a particularly eloquent description of the thrill of winning a bet; the knowledge that he read the race correctly, he had the skill and nerve to go against other peoples judgement and that ultimately the act of placing a winning bet provided a glow of self affirmation. Experienced gamblers will recognise this feeling; simply because we manage to pick the winner of the 3.30 at Thirsk then perhaps we can also perform well in other spheres of life that just 20 minutes ago seemed beyond us - trader of the year, managing director of a major PLC, a new life on the stage, and if time permits, possibly all three.

Unfortunately losses can bring an accompanied gloom that is as out of proportion to the ecstasy of winning. A losing betting slip can be casually tossed in the bin with the rest, (unless it is an unusually large bet that has gone down). With a spread bet where losses have unexpectedly ballooned, many of you will know the loss can be taken as a dark omen of oneís deeper failings - a sign of impending redundancy, rejection by oneís friends and family, swiftly followed by coma and death through starvation. And all because Leicester City got a fluky deflected goal in the 68th minute.

The subjective experience of losing will differ between spread account holders as will individual reactions to the progress of a bet. If you feel only the mildest form of disappointment from losing £500 in an afternoon (and more importantly, can afford it) then you appear to have the nerve to withstand the emotional rigours of Spread Betting. If however, you insist on going into a dark room to brood endlessly on your £50 reverse then you must seriously consider in future what degree of financial risk is acceptable on a bet without it ruining you and your familyís weekend.

The worst potential loss I ever faced was on a One Day International cricket game where I had bought the West Indies runs at 260. By coincidence a friend phoned and revealed that he had brought at precisely the same time which, as it transpired, was a poor decision on the part of both of us. Shortly after the trades, wickets began tumbling and Windies were reduced to 160 for 6. It was conceivable that the innings could close at around 180 leaving us with four figure losses. As we spoke another wicket fell. The particularly tragic aspect of the episode was the match wasnít even being covered on the radio, let alone terrestrial TV, so we were reduced to watching the constantly updated scoreboard provided by the Ceefax service. Deciding that bemoaning our luck over the telephone was doing the batsmen no good as their performance seemed to be getting worse as we spoke we hung up, leaving me concentrating on the Ceefax screen as the painfully slow progress of the batsmen scoring unfolded that mid-week evening.

When in the throes of great Spread Betting excitement a lot of people pace furiously around the room, shouting encouragement/threats at the participants. On this occasion, when things began to look really bad, and **I found myself become almost totally immobile**, unable to avert my eyes from the ëtotal runsí display at the bottom right hand corner of the screen and silently praying that the batsmenís name didnít change colour indicating that another wicket had fallen. After almost two hours of this exquisite agony, during which time I had just about managed to put the kettle on in a particularly ungainly way in order that I was still able to see the TV from the kitchen, the West Indies somehow managed to claw their way back into contention thanks to a tail-end half century. Though they did not win the match, they did manage to pass our buy target giving us a profit that in truth, was undeserved.

A single large loss certainly concentrates the mind somewhat. There is a potential pitfall for account holders approaching the cut-off day for finalising their account, whether this be weekly, bi-weekly of monthly. If one has sustained a loss in the accounting period so far it is all to easy to try and recoup these losses in a mad burst so that one can show a positive statement. This is a very poor tactic and is possibly the major cause of those hastily thought out trades one comes to regret very quickly.

For many, an almost mythical dimension is attached to the significance of winning/losing runs. Indeed these are at the heart of a number of totally unworkable betting ësystemsí. An average spread bettor will make a losing trade on slightly more occasions than he makes a profitable trade. As the margin on spread bets is 10% we can say that he would expect to win 45% of trades. It is all to easy to conceive of a pattern of results that appears to conform to this strike rate.

One might sense that wins and losses (of whatever magnitude) more or less follow one another in a uniform pattern (i.e. win, lose, win, lose, lose, win, win, lose). In fact the volatile way in which winning and losing exhibit themselves frequently seems to surprise people. Assuming a 45% win rate every bet stands a 1 in 10 chance of being the first in a row of four losers. Similarly every bet stands a 1 in 100 chance of being the first in a row of eight losers.

If you have three bets a week, totalling around 150 in a year, at some point you are almost certain to come across a substantial losing run of eight or more. Multiply eight by your average loss and you probably arrive at a scary looking figure. Again, assuming a win percentage of 45% this would mean that there was a 1 in 10 chance of a bet being the first of a winning run of three, and a 1 in 100 chance of a bet being the first in a winning run of six.

Even if it is unconscious, people tend to change their betting habits when facing winning/losing runs. Many subscribe to the theory of ëcrack on following wins - reign back following lossesí. Personally I tend to do the exact opposite, becoming tentative and betting smaller stakes when a winning run of more than four appears and taking the plunge more boldly should a series of losses rear its head. In fact both strategies are equally fallacious. **Reading anything into sequences is a waste of emotional effort, and any form of varying stakes according to a short term pattern of previous bets is equally futile.**

ëLuckí and ësuperstitioní play a significant part in the spread bettorís emotional outlook. Since a degree of pure chance is evident in all sporting events it is bound to impinge on Spread Betting. If you have calculated that the *Favourites Index* is, at 74 - 77, a couple of points above that of your estimates for the meeting causing you to sell then an eventual make-up of 10 is, in many respects, an outrageous piece of good fortune. Similarly a Test match washed out after the third day just after you bought the batting teamís runs is about as unfortunate as one can get. The trick is to accept these events as isolated and try not to ponder their higher significance.

The Spread Betting fraternity tends to be split into three types of personalities:

i)The Thrill Seekers

There are plenty of ways to win and lose money in a very short space of time on the spreads; these ëopportunitiesí attract those who like the feeling of a furious adrenaline rush. They are, from the point of view of the companies, the best clients. A gamble is not a gamble unless it is a large one and it may take ever-increasing stakes to produce the same buzz. A long drawn out event in which the result slowly becomes evident is unattractive to this breed- they much prefer the crucial ëdo or dieí moment to set the pulse racing.

The main difficulty with the long term financial prospects of the thrill seeker is that he is more concerned about spicing up sporting events with a wager than consistently making money from them. The spread companies are keen to promote markets that attract this type of punter. The ultimate thrill seekers ride is with markets where the spread is measured in seconds, for example, the number of seconds a boxing match lasts. Even the stately game of cricket isnít without its stomach churning markets. If you are so inclined you may bet on the out-come of the balls bowled in the first over of the test match. Thrill seekers pursue an entirely different betting philosophy to ëseriousí gamblers. They tend to be attracted by risk and seek out bets that are, by their nature, governed mostly by chance. This distinguishes them from the generally more successful gamblers who are mostly concerned about eliminating risk.

It would be easy to characterise the thrill seekers as bored city traders to whom Spread Betting losses are an insignificant problem. Indeed, the beginnings of the spread industry were very much geared to this type of client. Individuals of the next two categories can easily lapse into thrill seeking mode when there are no decent looking bets to oc-cupy them.

ii) The Sporting Know-Alls

It goes without saying that a certain degree of sporting knowledge is vital to stand a chance of profiting from Spread Betting, although I suspect that those who carry a wealth of sporting facts and figures in their brains do not necessarily make the best gamblers. It really comes down to the type of sporting knowledge one possesses. The ability to recite the Derby winners since 1950 may raise a few eyebrows down the local but carries little weight when considering a spread bet. I dare say a really excellent knowledge of the second string betting sports such as golf may put you at a considerable advantage. However, gener-ally the type of information that spread bettors need is so obtuse and specialised that it falls outside the normal limits of any conceivably ëinterestingí sporting facts.

I would have some difficulty naming the winner of last yearís Grand National, and the rules that govern the racehorse handicapping system are an utter mystery to me. I have, however, gained the not-particularly attractive ability to recall that ìon standard going in a non handicap race at Southwell, the average winning margin is 2.9 lengths, and as such ranks amongst the top 5 (in terms of winning distances) of all flat racing coursesî. As such this proudly places me in the third category of Spread Betting personality typesÖ

iii) The Anoraks

When the phrase ëprofessional gamblerí is uttered oneís mind tends to conjure up images of gauche wealth, cigars the size of baseball bats and private helicopters - along the lines of the image displayed by legendary gambler Terry Ramsden. Ramsden, in fact fell more accurately into the thrill seeker category and as such his huge gambling debts were his downfall. The true professional gambler tends to be pale and drawn from too much form book study and even if they are not walking encyclopaedias of sporting knowledge they are set in a professional gamblers way of thinking; considering accurately whether the odds on offer are in line with the true chance of the said event occurring. This may mean relating the current situation back to past results and involve some fairly serious study. This, more often than not leads to no actual bet being placed as genuine betting opportunities are few and far between.

Gamblers which straddle both the ëanoraksí and the ësporting know allísí category are probably the most dangerous types to the spread companies. Angus Loughran, famous as the anorak icon ëStattoí on Fantasy Football League fits into this niche. He is also a highly successful gambler and his comments in the press tend to be worth noting.

The Way to Go

For me, the gambling book with the best title must be Alan Pottsí *Against the Crowd*, his excellent view on tactics for betting on horses. Going ëagainst the crowdí seems to be the maxim for many successful gamblers, an ability to see through the inflated expectations for many competitors across a range of sports and know when to back against them.

In the UK we have a rather paradoxical attitude to sporting heroes. We love champions so long as they fit certain criteria; they must be exceptionally talented at their sport but with a habit of ignoring the technical textbooks. Ian Botham fits the bill here while Steve Davis certainly doesnít as he was perceived to be too ëperfectí. It helps if they are slightly eccentric and unchallenging. Frank Bruno...OK, Chris Eubank...less so. So opposing favourites can depend on whether they are favourites that the public want to win and want to bet on.

Manchester United are perhaps the most supported team in the world yet they are also the team that attracts the most ënegative feelingí (to try and adopt a fairly diplomatic phrase), amongst the uncommitted. Therefore an ëagainst the crowdí betting philosophy can frequently mean backing favourites though this appears to be contradictory. As a consequence I tend to find myself looking for any opportunity to back the ëunfashionableí favourites. I am always keen to go against the Brazilian football team, who despite doing nothing in World football of note for 20 years in the 70ís and 80ís still provided endless fodder for pundits marvelling at their ëremarkable ball skillsí and bendy free kicks.

Equally there exists ëfashionableí outsiders who are generally worth avoiding. Prior to World Cups a number of teams seem to show promise as good outsiders but have a tendency to fall flat on their face. Who can forget Peleís much discussed tip of Columbia for the 1994 tournament, who flopped in spectacular fashion. A number of European teams with excellent qualifying records always seem to catch the eye, Austria in 1990, Denmark in 1994. Yet the teams that outperform expectations generally seem to escape the attentions of the ëshrewdiesí looking for value outside the favourites.

The *Sporting Life* website bravely displays its record of recommended bets. As an exercise I split their recommendations into two categories. Firstly those which backed positive results - this would include buying the performance of the favourites, total goals, points, bookings, winning margins etc. There are one or two examples of ësellí bets which are ëpositivesí - selling the finishing positions in a tournament means that you are backing a competitor to do well, so this class of bets comes within this category.

The second category included all the ënegativeí bets in all the various markets. There are a number of bets which cannot be clearly called ëpositivesí or ënegativesí - the number of seconds a boxing match is an example; by selling duration of a fight you are in effect ëbuyingí the supremacy of the favourite as a good performance by the favourite will cause the fight to be end early. Any such bets I came across were ruled out of the equation.

Remarkably I found an enormous difference in the results between the two categories. The bets in the ënegativeí category were far more successful as those in the ëpositiveí category. Over 150 bets there was a loss of 251 points on the ëpositivesí but a profit of 87 on the ënegativesí. In the most recent month there was a profit of 146 for ënegativesí and a profit for 78 for the ëpositivesí. Almost twice as many *Sporting Life* bets were ëpositivesí than ënegativesí, and Iím sure this mirrors the betting habits of most account holders.

In terms of competitors performances we tend to look to back them to do well as in traditional fixed odds betting. There is also a tendency to shy away from selling certain variables. Many individuals would be wary of selling racing Starting Prices fearing the devastating consequences of a very long price winner; if one was to see a quote of 62 - 67 on the first 15 overs of a cricket innings the mind tends to instantly think in terms of the potential for a swashbuckling start with a flurry of boundaries contributing to a run rate of 10 per over.

The results of my look at the *Sporting Life* bets convinced me that at every opportunity the emphasis should be on looking for ënegativeí bets - i.e. precisely the types of wagers that other account holders do not seem generally comfortable with. I now pursue this angle relentlessly to the extent that only about 15% of my bets are ëpositivesí.

Appendix

It is often useful to convert fractional odds into their associated percentages. To do this there is a standard formula.

i)	Divide first number of odds by second number
ii)	Add one.
iii)	Divide result into 100

So for 6/4:
$6 \div 4 = 1.5$
$1.5 + 1 = 2.5$
$100 \div 2.5 = 40\%$

The following table gives the associated percentages for the most frequently used fractional odds:

Odds	Percentage	Odds	Percentage
2/9	81.83	6/4	40.00
1/4	80.00	13/8	38.10
1/3	75.00	7/4	36.36
4/11	73.33	15/8	34.78
2/5	71.43	2/1	33.33
4/9	69.23	11/5	31.25
1/2	66.67	9/4	30.77
8/15	65.22	12/5	29.41
4/7	63.64	5/2	28.57
8/13	61.90	11/4	26.67
4/6	60.00	3/1	25.00
8/11	57.89	10/3	23.08
4/5	55.56	7/2	22.22
5/6	54.55	4/1	20.00
10/11	52.38	9/2	18.18
Evs	50.00	5/1	16.67
11/10	47.62	11/2	15.38
6/5	45.45	6/1	14.29
5/4	44.44	13/2	13.33
11/8	42.11	7/1	12.50
		15/2	11.76